A Treasury of Timeless Truths

Enriching Insights from Scripture

Ben Godwin

A Treasury of Timeless Truths—Enriching Insights from Scripture

ISBN: 978-1-949297-86-7

Address all personal correspondence to:
Ben Godwin
P.O. Box 3161, Jasper, AL 35502
Email: Ben@bengodwin.org
Website: bengodwin.org

Individuals and church groups may order books from Ben Godwin directly, or from the publisher. Retailers and wholesalers should order from our distributors. Refer to the Deeper Revelation Books website for distribution information, as well as an online catalog of all our books.

Published by:
Deeper Revelation Books
Revealing "the deep things of God" (1 Cor. 2:10)
P.O. Box 4260, Cleveland, TN 37320 423-478-2843
Website: www.deeperrevelationbooks.org
Email: info@deeperrevelationbooks.org

Deeper Revelation Books assists Christian authors in publishing and distributing their books. Final responsibility for design, content, permissions, editorial accuracy, and doctrinal views, either expressed or implied, belongs to the author. We consider it a great honor and blessing to collaborate in projects intended to advance the kingdom of God.

Contents

PART 4
Inspired Insights on Various Biblical Themes

Dedication

James Raymond Bolton

August 22, 1934—July 26, 2020

Solomon observed, *"Most men will proclaim each his own goodness, but* ***who can find a faithful man****?"* (Pr. 20:6) It is a rare quality indeed, but I found a "faithful man" in Goodsprings, Alabama. He was my father-in-law and like a second father to me. Bro. Raymond was a coal miner by trade and a pastor by calling. He started playing the piano at age ten, and served as our church pianist for seventy-five years. He played and sang for several singing groups, including the Melody Aires and the Happy Goodmans before they were famous. He pastored our church—*Goodsprings Full Gospel Church*—for thirty-three years. After serving as his assistant pastor for five years, I became the lead pastor when he retired in 1999, and he was my assistant.

Faithfulness defined Raymond's life. He was a faithful worker for the Drummond Coal Company for forty-four years, rarely ever missing a shift.

Whenever he was laid off, he cut meat as a butcher in local grocery stores. He was faithful to his wife, Faye, for forty-six years until her passing in 2007. He was faithful to our church long before and after he was the pastor. He seldom missed a service until his health failed at the age of eighty-five. Most of all, he was faithful to the call of God. After he retired from pastoring, he continued in music ministry and volunteered at a local food bank. He was a role model of Christian love and selfless giving to our church and community.

Bro. Raymond could have been a rich man if he wasn't so generous. He grew huge gardens just so he could give food away. He raised chickens and supplied many neighbors with fresh eggs. He raised cows for milk and beef. He was a great cook and loved to bake cakes to give away. Actually, he was rich—rich in love, faith, prayer, and other things money can't buy. He laid up treasure in heaven with his good works.

Raymond Bolton was truly a remarkable man. It is impossible to replace a man of his stature. There is a huge vacancy in our family, church, and community since his passing. It was an honor to serve with this great man of God. It was a privilege to be his son-in-law, assistant pastor, then pastor, and his friend. We honor the anointed gift God placed in his life. We continue his legacy by building on the firm foundation he laid. We loved him deeply and miss him dearly. As a song he loved to play and sing says, we will "meet you in the morning."

Introduction

For over a decade, I have had the privilege of writing a monthly column for the Religion/Faith page of our county-wide newspaper in Jasper, Alabama—*The Daily Mountain Eagle.* Most of these columns are spinoffs of sermons I've preached in our local congregation—*Goodsprings Full Gospel Church.* These messages were modified and condensed to an article size and format to run in our newspaper. Then they were posted on our websites and on social media to maximize readership. Many of these columns have also been posted on *Charisma Magazine's* website (charismamag.com) as well to reach an even wider audience.

The downside of printed articles is they are often read one time and forgotten or discarded. Digital articles posted on websites and social media are easily overlooked or difficult to retrieve when you wish to re-read them later. Thus, the purpose of this book—to provide a permanent resource people can read and then easily access over and over again.

This book is divided into four sections: *Inspired Insights on Victorious Living, Inspired Insights on Social Issues, Inspired Insights on Jesus' Ministry,* and *Inspired Insights on Various Biblical Themes.* Each chapter contains a complete thought so you can read them in any order. Also, each chapter is short enough to read in a single setting (averaging

1,000-1,400 words). So, you can use it for devotional purposes and read one chapter per day or you can use it as a topical, Bible study. Preachers and Bible teachers are welcome and encouraged to use any of this material in your own message preparations. As Charles Spurgeon observed, "All originality and no plagiarism makes for dull preaching."[1] We all borrow and learn from others so feel free to borrow and share.

One thing is certain, each chapter contains an inspired message from God. As D. L. Moody said, "I know the Bible is inspired because it inspires me."[2] The following pages are words God has breathed into my spirit as I studied, meditated, and prayed over His inspired Word. It is my sincere prayer that God will speak to you in a personal way through the *logos* (written Word) and the *rhema* (living Word) as you read these pages. May the Lord impart to you fresh wisdom, insight, inspiration, and new perspective. May He breathe fresh life into your spirit as you feast on this fresh, heavenly manna. Truly, the bread of life never goes stale.

Jesus compared the kingdom of heaven to hidden treasure buried in a field (Mt. 13:44). Something hidden must be discovered. The Bible is a treasure trove of timeless, transforming truths. It is loaded with divinely inspired nuggets of wisdom that have the power to greatly enrich and enhance every aspect of your life. Like precious and priceless gemstones, these cherished concepts aren't typically seen sitting on the surface, easily discovered by the casual Bible reader. Those who want more must dig down deep to find the hidden treasures in Scripture—God's glorious gold mine. As one author noted, "No one ever graduates from Bible study until he meets its Author face to face."[3] So, grab a shovel, fellow prospectors, and let's dig deep, expecting to strike a mother lode of rich, golden truths together.

—Ben Godwin

PART 1

INSPIRED INSIGHTS ON VICTORIOUS LIVING

CHAPTER 1

Champions R US in Christ

Nowhere in the Bible are we called losers, failures, or underdogs. Rather, God's people are described as victorious winners! *"The Lord will make you the head and not the tail; you shall be above only, and not be beneath"* (Dt. 28:13). 2 Corinthians 2:14 declares, *"Now thanks be unto God, which always leads us in triumph in Christ."* The Apostle Paul called us "more than conquerors" and the Apostle John used the term "overcomers" repeatedly. So, there's a champion in all of us that needs to be developed and released.

Surprisingly, the word "champion" is only used three times in Scripture, all in reference to Goliath, the Philistine giant from Gath (1 Sam. 17:4, 23, 51). Goliath means "exile" and is a fitting type of Satan who was exiled from heaven. A champion is "a person who has defeated all opponents in a competition so as to hold first place."[4] To be the best you have to beat the best. To be a champion you have to beat the champion. David defeated this pagan champion and became God's champion. David is a type of Christ who defeated Satan, the champion of evil.

Just as every Israelite became winners when David slew Goliath, all Christians share in Christ's victory over Satan on the cross. Even as David killed Goliath with his own sword, Jesus took the devil's biggest weapon (death) and defeated him with it—"*That through death he might destroy him that had the power of death, that is, the devil; and deliver them who through fear of death were all their lifetime subject to bondage*" (Heb. 2:14-15, KJV). God is raising up an army of spiritual champions of faith in these last days.

The New Testament writers used a familiar word to describe God's people—*Nike* (pronounced nee-kay). Centuries before the Nike swoosh symbol became one of the most recognizable fashion brands in the world, Paul and John used that term to describe victorious Christians. Different forms of the root word that *Nike* comes from mean "victory, victorious, to subdue, to conquer, overcome, prevail, or to get the victory."[5] In Greek mythology, *Nike* is the goddess of victory. She supposedly gave victory in battle or sports competitions. When the Greeks won their battles, they thanked *Ares* (their god of war) and *Nike* (their goddess of victory). When we win our spiritual battles, we give thanks to the one, true, Almighty God—Jehovah/Yahweh.

The New Testament uses the Greek word *Nike* over thirty times. Even Jesus used it. For example, He said, *"In the world you will have tribulation: but be of good cheer; I have* ***overcome*** [*nikao*] *the world"* (Jn. 16:33). *Nikao*, the verb form of the same root word *Nike* comes from, means "to vanquish beyond, to gain a decisive victory, or to conquer."[6]

The Apostle John used *Nike* many times in his writings. Wherever you see the words "overcome(s)" or "overcame" (or "overcometh" in the KJV), it is translated from the Greek word *nikao*. For instance, *"I write to you, young men, because you have* ***overcome*** *the wicked one ... I have written to you, young men, because you are strong, and the word of God abides in you, and you have* ***overcome*** *the wicked one"* (1 Jn. 2:13-14).

Here are some other examples: *"You are of God, little children, and have* ***overcome*** *them, because He who is in you is greater than he who is in the world"* (1 Jn. 4:4). *"For whatever is born of God* ***overcomes*** *the world. And this is the victory that has* ***overcome*** *the world—our faith. Who is he who* ***overcomes*** *the world, but he who believes that Jesus is the Son of God?"* (1 Jn. 5:4-5)

In the Book of Revelation, Jesus issued eight promises to the overcomers (Rev. 2:7, 11, 17, 26; 3:5, 12, 21; 21:7). In each instance, as John recorded it, he used the Greek word *nikao* which is translated "overcomes." Then John wrote of the saints' ultimate triumph over the great red dragon (Satan), *"And they* ***overcame*** *him by the blood of the Lamb, and by the word of their testimony; and they loved not their lives unto the death"* (Rev. 12:11). Notice it is in the past tense instead of the future tense. Why? Because we are not fighting to obtain the victory; we are fighting to maintain the victory! Jesus won the victory for us 2,000 years ago on the cross when He conquered sin, Satan, death, and hell. Victory for the child of God is not just a future hope, it is an established fact, a present-day reality! Because Christ overcame, we are overcomers too.

Paul also used another form of *Nike* in his writings. Concerning the resurrection and the believer's triumph over death, he used the Greek word *nikos* (pronounced nee-kos), translated "victory" three times in one passage. He wrote, *"So when this corruptible has put on incorruption, and this mortal has put on immortality, then shall be brought to pass the saying that is written: 'Death is swallowed up in* ***victory****.' 'O Death, where is your sting? O Hades, where is your* ***victory****?' ... But thanks be to God, who gives us the* ***victory*** *through our Lord Jesus Christ"* (1 Cor. 15:54-55, 57). God has made us victorious overcomers through Christ. We can now live in *Nike* (victory) in every area of life because Christ has won the *Nike* (victory).

Then Paul raised the bar even higher by using another Greek word to describe us despite all the dangers we face. *"Nay, in all these things we are* ***more than conquerors*** *through him that loved us"* (Rom. 8:37, KJV). One Greek word (*hypernikaō*, pronounced hoop-er-nik-ah-o) is translated into the phrase "more than conquerors."[7] Paul was basically saying we are super champions! *Hypernikaō* was a term used for Caesar. The foot soldiers in his army would fight his battles and win the victory. They were conquerors. Caesar gave the orders and the victory was brought back to him. He was more than a conqueror. To use a modern illustration, a heavy weight boxer who fights for twelve rounds and is declared the winner is a conqueror. His wife, who doesn't even break a sweat watching the bout on TV, greets him at the door with a kiss, and takes the prize check, is more than a conqueror. You see, Jesus won the battle and gave us (His bride) the prize!

As an old song says, "We've been made more than conquerors, overcomers in this life. We've been made victorious, through the blood of Jesus Christ." Jesus conquered sin, Satan, and self. He defeated death, hell, and the grave for us by His *Nike* (victory) on the cross. So, whenever you see a *Nike* swoosh symbol, don't just think of trendy sportswear. Let it be a reminder of the *Nike* (victory) Jesus won on the cross and gave to us. Besides, we don't need a pair of expensive athletic shoes to be a champion. We are all champions by faith in Christ—the ultimate champion.

CHAPTER 2

From the Underdog to the Top Dog

We all love rags-to-riches and tragedy-to-triumph stories, right? We're inspired when someone overcomes overwhelming odds and obstacles to rise to the top. We cheer when an unknown underdog upsets a favored champion. The Bible contains many stories of God using unlikely underdogs to win great victories. *"The Lord will make you the head and not the tail; you shall be above only, and not be beneath"* (Dt. 28:13). Modern translation: "I'll take you from being the underdog and make you the top dog!"

An underdog is "a person or team who is expected to lose in a contest or conflict."[8] The ancient Israelites were serious underdogs against their nemesis—the Philistines. Backslidden King Saul ignored the Prophet Samuel. Outnumbered, they had just lost a big battle and morale was low in Israel's army (1 Sam. 13). The Philistines had a big military advantage, but Israel had a spiritual advantage—they served Jehovah God not false idols.

Against all odds, Jonathan and his armor bearer attacked (two against hundreds). There was no way they should have survived much less won this battle. Jonathan was either courageous or crazy or both. He boldly stated, "*Come, let us go over to the garrison of these uncircumcised; it may be that the Lord will work for us. For nothing restrains the Lord from saving by many or by few*" (1 Sam. 14:6). Israel won a great victory because two guys dared to act in faith. God turned the underdogs into top dogs.

Perhaps you've heard the amazing story about Rich Strike, the horse that won the 2022 Kentucky Derby. Do yourself a favor, google it, and watch the replay. Rich Strike won a $1.86 million prize. He only got in the race because the 20th horse had to withdraw at the last minute. He started from the worst position on the outside of the track. He maneuvered his way through the field of nineteen other horses from the back. His jockey, Sonny Leon, had never been to the Kentucky Derby. His trainer, Eric Reed, had never raced a horse in the Derby. His owner, Richard Dawson, bought him for $30,000 (peanuts for racehorses). He was one of the biggest long shots to ever win the race, with 80-1 closing odds. Yet Rich Strike outran million-dollar steeds to win on the grandest stage.[9] The underdog (horse) became the top dog!

The Bible records the greatest underdog story in history—David versus Goliath. Goliath was an oversized ogre at 9 feet, 6 inches tall. To put that in perspective, NBA All-Star Shaquille O'Neal is listed at 7'1," Andre the Giant was 7'4," and the tallest man recorded in the Guinness Book of World Records, Robert Wadlow, was measured at 8'11." Goliath was so big people thought he couldn't lose. David thought he was so big he couldn't miss! Oddly, David brought five rocks to a sword fight. Some say it was extra ammunition in case he missed. Others see it as an act of faith—one stone for Goliath and four for his brothers/sons he would fight later (2 Sam. 21:16-18, 1 Chr. 20:4-8). You see, life is a series of battles. You're either in a battle, fresh out of a battle, or about to face another one. David believed God would not only help him bring Goliath down but every other giant he had to face!

One Hebrew word for "giant" is *nephil* (plural is *nephilim*) meaning "a bully or a tyrant."[10] All giants in the Bible were enemies of Israel. Goliath was a big bully barking out blasphemy against God and terrorizing Israel. Satan is also a bully who tries to intimidate us, but *"If God be for us, who can be against us?"* (Rom. 8:31) David stunned Goliath with a stone to his skull. Then he took his own sword and decapitated him. With their champion dead, the Philistines fled. That day the world witnessed God take an underdog and make him the top dog.

What about Gideon's 300-man, underdog army? The Midianites invaded Israel like a swarm of grasshoppers. God let them oppress His people for their chronic idolatry. The Israelites survived by hiding in caves. The enemy swooped in at harvest time and destroyed their crops causing a dire food shortage. On the brink starvation, Israel desperately cried out to God for help. Then God raised up another unlikely underdog to deliver them—Gideon. Hungry and scared, Gideon was hiding behind a wine press threshing wheat to make bread when an angel appeared saying, "*The Lord is with you, you mighty man of valor*" (Jgs. 6:12). Gideon sure didn't look like a hero; he looked like a wimp, a coward, and a chicken! He made this excuse, "*O my Lord, how can I save Israel? Indeed, my clan is the weakest in Manasseh, and I am the least in my father's house*" (Jgs. 6:15). Talk about an underdog, Gideon was a nobody going nowhere. But God saw his potential.

Gideon blew a trumpet to rally the troops and 32,000 men showed up. Not bad! However, there were 135,000 Midianites soldiers so they were outnumbered 4-1. God said there were too many men and Gideon dismissed the fearful. His army shrank by 2/3rds as 22,000 went home. With 10,000 men left, they were outnumbered 13-1 and God said, "*The people are still too many.*" So, God tested them at the water and sent 9,700 more men home leaving a puny, 300-man army. They were outnumbered 450-1. Did someone say underdogs? At God's order, they snuck into the Midianite camp at night and all 300 men simultaneously blew trumpets, broke clay pitchers, waved torches, and shouted, "*The sword of the Lord and of Gideon*" (Jgs. 7:20). The Midianites woke up out of a dead sleep terrified and panicked. In the chaos, they scattered and started slaying each other. Israel miraculously defeated the Midianites and God turned a band of underdogs into top dogs.

Finally, there is the woman Jesus called a dog—the Syrophoenician Woman (Mt. 15:22-28). She begged Jesus to deliver her demonized daughter. At first, Jesus ignored her—"*He answered her not a word.*" Tough luck, lady! The disciples asked Jesus to send her away but she was persistent. "*Then she came and worshipped him, saying, Lord, help me.*" Then Jesus, it seems, insulted her, "*It is not good to take the children's bread and throw it to the* ***little dogs****.*" She was Greek (Mk. 7:26) and Gentiles were often called "dogs" and considered unclean by Jews. If she was a dog, she must have been a bulldog because she wouldn't take no for an answer. She humbly replied, "*Yes, Lord: yet even the* ***little dogs*** *eat the crumbs which fall from their masters' table.*" Wow! Jesus was so impressed by her response, He said, "*O woman, great is your faith! Let it be to you as you desire.*" (Incidentally, the only two people

Jesus said had great faith were both Gentiles, the Centurion and this woman.) She was an underdog but when Jesus answered her plea and delivered her daughter, she was a top dog!

Friend, you may feel like an underdog today facing overwhelming odds, but God can turn your situation around 180 degrees overnight. He promised to *"make you the head and not the tail; you shall be above only, and not be beneath."* Trust in Him to turn yet another underdog into a top dog. HOWL-lelujah!

Chapter 3

Strength in the Struggle

We all like the easy button. We all want this year to be easier, better, and more normal than the recent past. The last few years brought a lot of challenges, changes, interruptions, and inconveniences (masks, long lines, higher prices, shortages of food, money, and other products). There was a lot of social, political, and financial upheaval. It challenged our comfort zones, stretched our faith, and made us pray and depend on God more than ever. Face it, we don't like change. Truly, the only people who like change are wet babies!

In August of 2005, Staples introduced the "easy button"—a novelty item for offices as a fun way to relieve stress. Pushing the button causes it to say, "That was easy." Staples has sold over eight million Easy Buttons, with proceeds going toward the Special Olympics. It served as a symbol of the frustrations and challenges of small business. It was a clever ad campaign as they tried to make things easier for their customers.[11] We all like quick fixes and shortcuts. We all want to wave a magic wand and "poof" make everything better faster. But life often doesn't work that way. Real life is hard sometimes, and we must plod and plow through it. Some things we don't enjoy, but we must simply endure. The Bible doesn't say that life or faith will be easy. Jesus never promised trouble-free living. In fact, He predicted the opposite—*"In the world you will have tribulation; but be of good cheer, I have overcome the world"* (Jn. 16:33). The Psalmist provided this reality check and promise, *"Many are the afflictions of the righteous, but the Lord delivers him out of them all"* (Ps. 34:19).

So, why is life such a struggle? Because there is a constant tug-of-war between good and evil, God and Satan, truth and error, light and darkness, the spirit and the flesh. These forces keep clashing in a series of struggles. God gives us grace to face our struggles and makes us stronger by them. Someone said, "Where there is no struggle, there is no strength."[12] The struggle we are in today is developing the strength we need for tomorrow. Plainly put, if God removed all our struggles, we wouldn't grow!

To struggle means "to contend with an adversary, opposing force, task, or problem."[13] Remember the old saying, "What doesn't kill you makes you stronger"? Well, then we should be super strong by now, right? Strength is built through resistance. Athletes who use weights for training in their sport build muscle and strength by resisting (pushing against) the weights. The same is true for us spiritually. James 4:7 instructs us to *"Submit to God.* ***Resist*** *the devil and he will flee from you."* The more we resist Satan, sin, and self, the stronger we become. Consider the following:

- As a butterfly struggles to break out of a cocoon, its wings develop so it can fly.
- As a bird or reptile breaks out of an egg, it gets stronger to face bigger challenges ahead.
- As an eagle fights against opposing air currents, it learns to soar higher.
- As a salmon swims against rapids and even jumps waterfalls, it elevates itself to higher spawning pools.
- As a baby squeezes through the birth canal, amniotic fluid is forced out of its lungs so it can breathe.
- As a toddler strains to crawl, pull up, and roll over, it builds muscles to later walk and run.
- As a student studies for assignments and tests, he or she learns and finds the tassel is worth the hassle on graduation day.

You see, we can't have a testimony without a test. We can't have victory without a battle. We can't be overcomers if there's nothing to overcome. Remember, every miracle in the Bible first started as a problem. Impossibilities with men are opportunities to God. The Christian life is a struggle because we are going against the grain of what is popular in our corrupt culture. Any dead fish can float downstream, but it takes someone with guts and grit to go against the current.

Jesus empowered His disciples to endure the struggle as He sent them out as lambs among wolves (Mt. 10:1). He warned them that the road would not be easy. He prepared them (and us) to face the struggle of rejection (Mt. 10:12-15), religious and political persecution (vs. 16-20), betrayal by family (v. 21), and demonic hatred (v. 22). Then He emphasized, *"But he who* ***endures to the end*** *will be saved."* Paul echoed that sentiment when he wrote, *"You therefore must* ***endure hardship*** *as a good soldier of Jesus Christ"* (2 Tim. 2:3). The Christian life is more like living on a battleship than a luxury cruise liner. Soft saints won't survive severe spiritual warfare. We must be tough enough to endure temptation (Jam. 1:12) and to *"run with endurance the race that is set before us"* (Heb. 12:1).

The Christian race is not a short sprint; it's a long-distance marathon. It's not about who starts the fastest; it's about who finishes the race. We should strive to finish strong like the Apostle Paul who wrote, *"I have fought the good fight, I have finished the race, I have kept the faith"* (2 Tim. 4:7). In Aesop's famous fable, the hare sped ahead to gain a big lead, but then he got lazy and took a nap. Meanwhile, the tortoise crept along (steady Eddie) and passed him. The hare woke up just in time to see the tortoise cross the finish line. Slow and steady wins the race. It may not seem like you're making much spiritual progress, but keep striving, soldier, you're getting stronger every day! Every struggle in life only serves to make you stronger.

CHAPTER 4

Victory Even in Your Valleys

Life is full of peaks and valleys, ups and downs, highs and lows. While we'd love to live on the mountaintop all the time, that's not reality. You will face some dark valleys in life, so don't be surprised or despair. We all experience disappointments, failure, betrayal, conflict, broken relationships, financial stress, and the loss of loved ones. That's not negativism—that's realism! We all deal with negative thoughts and emotions, but we must keep walking by faith, not by our feelings. Emotions fluctuate like a Yo-Yo, but our devotion must remain constant.

Jesus never promised trouble-free living. In fact, He predicted the opposite (Jn. 16:33). In this fallen world, bad things happen to good people, and sometimes the righteous suffer and the wicked prosper (Mt. 5:45). Life is not always fair or fun, but God is still faithful. Valleys are spiritually symbolic of trials and tribulations. Peter reminded us, *"Beloved, do not think it strange concerning the fiery trial which is to try you, as though some strange thing happened to you; but rejoice to the extent that you partake of Christ's sufferings"* (1 Pt. 4:12-13a).

Valleys are low places. Occasionally, we get down emotionally and even spiritually, but we must not stay down. Solomon wrote of Jesus, *"I am ... the lily of the valleys"* (Song. 2:1). Notice it's plural. We can make it through every valley we face knowing He is with us. The ancient Syrians miscalculated—*"Thus says the Lord: 'Because the Syrians have said, "The Lord is God of the hills, but He is not God of the valleys," therefore I will deliver all this great multitude into your hand, and you shall know that I am the Lord'"* (1 Kgs. 20:28). God helped Israel defeat Syria just to prove that He was with them on the mountains and in their valleys, too. Consider eight significant valleys in Scripture:

- **The Valley of Baca:** *"Blessed is the man ... who passing through the valley of Baca make*[s] *it a well"* (Ps. 84:5-6, KJV). Baca means "weeping" or "sorrow."[14] Baca refers to a type of "weeping" tree; that is, one that drips resin or gum-like tears, such as a balsam, mulberry, or aspen tree. We can't fully experience God's comfort until we first deal with grief. When David's city, Ziklag, was burned, and he and his men's wives and children were captured, they wept until they couldn't weep anymore. Then they blamed David and wanted to stone him. *"But David encouraged himself in the Lord his God"* (1 Sam. 30:6, KJV), and they pursued after the enemy and recovered everything they lost. The figurative valley of Baca became a well of blessing. We all experience times of sorrow, but God can turn it around in our favor—*"Weeping may endure for a night, but joy comes in the morning"* (Ps. 30:5).

- **The Valley of Elah:** This valley, meaning "oak,"[15] is where David fought Goliath (1 Sam. 17:2-10). After being anointed by Samuel, chosen by God as king, and playing his harp in the royal court, David faced his fiercest foe in this deadly valley. David stood strong and tall like an oak tree and God turned his biggest battle into his greatest victory! The harp player became a giant slayer in the Valley of Elah.
- **The Valley of the Shadow of Death:** *"Yea, though I walk through the valley of the shadow of death, I will fear no evil; for You are with me"* (Ps. 23:4). Other versions render it, "the darkest valley." The Hebrew word for "shadow of death" is *sal-ma-wet*, which means "darkness" or "dark shadows." It contains the same root as the Hebrew word for "death" (*ma-wet*), so it is easy to see why some Bible translators include

the mention of death in Psalm 23:4. The Psalmist encountered many dark valleys when King Saul tried to kill him, gave his wife (Michal) to another man, and chased him as a fugitive for years. God kept David through all the perils and lonely nights of hiding in caves. All along, he was training for reigning. As Kelly Willard's song states, "Hidden valleys turn shepherds into kings."

- **The Valley of Berachah:** This was the site where Jehoshaphat defeated the Moabites and Ammonites. He placed the singers and musicians in front of the army and, while they worshipped, God ambushed the enemy presumably with angelic warriors. Before the conflict, Jahaziel prophesied, "*The battle is not yours, but God's … You will not need to fight in this battle. Position yourselves, stand still and see the salvation of the Lord*" (2 Chr. 20:15b, 17a). They named this valley "Berachah" (or "blessing") because it took three days to collect all the spoils of war (2 Chr. 20:25-26). God turned their biggest battle into their biggest blessing!
- **The Valley Full of Ditches:** When Israel and Judah fought against the Moabites, they traveled through the desert and couldn't find any water for seven days. Facing dehydration and certain death, Jehoshaphat called on the prophet Elisha who told them

to dig ditches throughout the valley. Those who expect God's blessings must prepare room for them. Then God supernaturally filled the ditches with water. When the Moabites saw the reddish sunlight reflect on the water in the ditches, they thought it was blood. So, they assumed the Israeli army had been slain and they were free to take the spoils of war. Instead, the Israelites surprised and attacked the Moabites and God gave them a great victory, and turned their water shortage into a water surplus overnight (2 Kgs. 3:16-24).

- **The Valley of Hinnom:** Hinnom was an ancient site of pagan rituals, Baal worship, and human sacrifice (2 Chr. 28:1-4; 33:6-9). The Greek term *Gehenna* means "the vale of Hinnom" or the "valley of Hinnom." In Jesus' time, it was the garbage dump of Jerusalem where trash was burned, and corpses of animals and criminals were discarded.[16] *Gehenna* is translated "hell" twelve times in the New Testament. Jesus used this analogy in His preaching (Mt. 5:22, 29-30; 10:28). While hell is a literal place, we often use the term figuratively to express going through hellish situations. Winston Churchill said, "If you're going through hell, keep going."[17] If you're facing hell on earth, call on the One who can bring heaven down into your situation.

- **The Valley of Dry Bones:** God gave Ezekiel a vivid vision of a mass graveyard of scattered skeletons (chapter 37). Suddenly, the bones reconnected, sinew and skin covered them, and the corpses resurrected as an "exceeding great army." This army represented "the whole house of Israel" and how spiritual revival would come. This speaks of how God can bring life out of death. Just as the Holy Spirit raised Christ from the grave, He can breathe new life into our dead circumstances (Rom. 8:11). God is bringing the church out of the Valley of Dry Bones (dead religion), raising up another mighty army, and breathing new life into His people in these last days.
- **The Valley of Jehoshaphat:** Jehoshaphat means "Jehovah is Judge."[18] God, not man, is our judge and He has the final verdict in our lives. This valley is also called "the valley of decision" (Jl. 3:2, 12-14). Sometimes decisions can be difficult and stressful, but God can bring peace and clear direction to our decision-making. Our destiny is not a matter of chance, but a matter of choice. God has the final say in the affairs of men. Valleys often help to push us into making decisions that propel us toward God's purpose and destiny in our lives.

So, if you find yourself in a low place, remember it is temporary. We go through valleys; we don't live in them permanently. The "Lily of Valleys" is with you, and He will give you victory even in your valleys.

CHAPTER 5

Conviction or Condemnation?

One of the Devil's biggest weapons in his bag of dirty tricks is condemnation. To condemn means "to pronounce to be guilty, to sentence to punishment, or to pass judgment against."[19] Satan is called the "accuser of the brethren" (Rev. 12:10). He and his demons are like prosecutors who find fault, point the finger of blame, accuse us of guilt, and they want to impose the death penalty. Notice their sly tactic. First, they entice us to sin. Then, if we do sin, they jump on our back and condemn us for doing what they suggested all along. What diabolical tacticians they are!

The good news is that Jesus is our Advocate, our defense attorney. *"My little children, these things I write to you, so that you may not sin. And if anyone sins, we have an* ***Advocate*** *with the Father, Jesus Christ the righteous"* (1 Jn. 2:1). The Greek word *parakletos* translated "advocate" here is also translated "Comforter" four times in reference to the Holy Spirit (Jn. 14:6, 26; 15:26, 16:7).[20] So, Christ is our Advocate and the Holy Spirit is our Comforter. They both stand by our side to defend us. That means we have double representation. If you're in legal trouble, it's good to have a lawyer; it's even better to have two. Defense attorneys do everything they can to prove their clients are innocent even if they know they're guilty. Well, I confess I am guilty as charged—*"For all have sinned and fall short of the glory of God"* (Rom. 3:23).

Truly, we are all guilty, but because of faith, confession, repentance, and forgiveness, the blood of Jesus is admitted to the court as evidence in our favor. We have been exonerated. The Judge, our Heavenly Father, has already declared us "Not guilty!" if we claim what is rightfully ours. This court is rigged in our favor and this case is dismissed. Hallelujah! So, when demons remind you of your past, remind them of their past (it's a lot worse than yours). They're the ones who rebelled against God, were expelled from heaven, and corrupted the human race with sin. Better yet, when they remind you of your past, remind them of their future! Case closed!

Some amputees experience what is known as "phantom pain." They feel pain in a limb that is no longer attached to their body. This is a cruel trick of the nervous system and the brain. Condemnation is like phantom pain. The devil wants you to feel anguish over your past sins that don't even exist anymore. If you have repented and been forgiven, those sins have been obliterated by the blood of Jesus. *"As far as the east is from the west, so far has* ***He removed our transgressions*** *from us"* (Ps. 103:12). *"Their sins and iniquities will I remember no more"* (Heb. 10:17, KJV). No wonder the songwriter penned, "My sin, oh, the bliss of this glorious thought, my sin, not in part but the whole, is nailed to the cross, and I bear it no more, praise the Lord, it is well with my soul."

Like most kids, I was afraid of the dark. When my mom tucked me in at night, the shadows in my room played tricks on my mind. I was sure that if I hung my foot over the side of the bed, a boogie monster would eat it off. Shadows in the closet were evil ogres ready to devour me. I would panic and cry for Mom. She'd turn the light on, open the closet, look under the bed, and show me it was all just my imagination. That's what condemnation is—a figment of our imagination. All we must do is turn on the light of God's Word and the sinister shadows will vanish.

The word "condemn" also means "to judge unfit for use or service."[21] For instance, if the health department condemns a dilapidated house, it is declared unfit for occupancy. That's the enemy's goal with condemnation—to declare us unfit for use. Demons whisper in our ear, "You've failed too many times, God won't forgive you, you're unworthy, He'll never use you again." Remember, the devil is a liar (Jn. 8:44). *"There is therefore now* ***no condemnation*** *to them which are in Christ Jesus, who walk not after the flesh, but after the spirit"* (Rom 8:1). "Walking after the spirit" doesn't mean you are perfect; it simply means you are striving to please God.

So, what is the difference between conviction and condemnation?

- Conviction is from God (accept it); condemnation is from Satan (reject it).
- Conviction leads you to repentance; condemnation drives you to despair.
- Conviction inspires you to keep striving; condemnation tells you to quit.
- Conviction says God will help you; condemnation says there's no hope for you.
- Conviction shows you the answer; condemnation only shows you the problem.
- Conviction helps you change; condemnation says it's permanent.

The big difference between the two is obvious in Peter and Judas. Conviction drove Peter to repentance; condemnation drove Judas to suicide! They both failed and committed similar sins. Peter cursed and denied Jesus; Judas betrayed Him for thirty pieces of silver (the paltry price of a slave). Judas could have been forgiven and restored if he had repented. Instead, he listened to the voice of condemnation and was doomed (Mt. 27:3-5). Peter was restored, reinstated, and about fifty-four days later, preached on the Day of Pentecost and 3,000 souls were saved (Ac. 2:14-41). He went on to become a prominent leader in the New Testament Church.

Condemnation screams, "You're nothing but a hypocrite, you've failed too many times, God will never forgive you. You're a disgrace, you might as well quit praying and going to church. You're unworthy, go ahead and indulge in sin. Why don't you just give up and end it all. God will never use you again."

Conviction says, "Yes, you've failed, but repent and keep striving to please God. You can be forgiven, renewed, and restored. Every day is a new beginning in Christ, you are a new creature in Him. Yes, you're unworthy, but His blood makes you worthy. There's no sin too big for the blood of Jesus and no failure too great for God's grace to overcome." 1 John 3:20 reassures, *"For **if our heart condemns us**, God is greater than our heart, and knows all things."* Jesus showed us the perfect balance between loving sinners without condoning sin when He said, *"Neither do I condemn you; go and sin no more"* (Jn. 8:11). Conviction or condemnation, to which voice will you listen?

Chapter 6

Running for Refuge

David is the most prominent Bible character besides Jesus. His name, mentioned 1,139 times in the KJV, means "beloved."[22] He was loved by God and still is by millions of Bible readers inspired by his story. But not everyone loved him. He was hated by some of his own brothers, his father-in-law, King Saul, and all the enemies of Israel. God's favor on David's life provoked jealousy and placed a bullseye on his back. Jesus warned His chosen disciples, *"You will be hated by all for My name's sake. But he who endures to the end will be saved"* (Mt. 10:22). We can endure being the target of hell's hatred when we know we're the focus of heaven's love.

Imagine David's emotional roller coaster ride. When this harp player turned giant slayer killed Goliath, he went from a lifelong zero to an instant hero. The farm boy from obscurity became an overnight celebrity. God promoted him from the pasture to palace (2 Sam. 7:8). He was appointed captain of Saul's army and ate caviar in the castle. He was living like royalty when, suddenly, the red carpet was jerked out from under him. His dream turned into a nightmare. Saul's insane jealousy became a sinister obsession to destroy him. As quickly as David became the most famous face in Israel, Saul vilified him as public enemy number one. He nursed a vicious vendetta against him and threw his spear at David three different times to kill him, but each time he escaped (1 Sam. 18:11; 19:10). Saul put a bounty on his head, mounted a massive manhunt, and chased him as a fugitive for years. Our adversary and his demonic minions seek to destroy us daily too (1 Pt. 5:8), but God's hand is a supernatural shield around us (Ps. 5:12).

David, then an outlaw, ran for his life hiding in woods and caves (1 Sam. 23:14). We are all running somewhere. When the going gets tough, we will either run toward God or away from God for refuge. When life is unfair, people mistreat you, and the enemy attacks you from all sides, where do you run for refuge? The old hymn still rings true, "*Where could I go? O where could I go? Seeking a refuge for my soul. Needing a Friend to help me in the end, where could I go but to the Lord?*" David ran to five specific people or places which are all spiritually significant:

1. **David ran to the prophet Samuel in Ramah**—1 Sam. 19:18-24. What a perfect person and place to run to in a crisis. Ramah, which means "height" or "elevated," was a town full of prophets, so David ran to the prophet of God (who had anointed him to be the next king earlier) for prayer and advice. When you're facing a trial, get in God's presence and around anointed people who can pray you through to victory. Don't withdraw into a shell and isolate yourself. Find other believers to stand with you and support you. There's power in partnership with anointed people.
2. **David ran to his best friend, Jonathan**—1 Sam. 20:1. They were brothers-in-law, but closer than actual blood brothers. Jonathan, meaning "the Lord has given,"[23] was a spiritual friend who "strengthened his hand in God" (1 Sam. 23:16). He saw God's favor on David and was supportive and not envious of his success. They were BFFs—"*The soul of Jonathan was knit to the soul of David, and Jonathan loved him as his own soul*" (1 Sam. 18:1). Earlier, Jonathan made a covenant with David and gave him his royal robe, sword, bow, and belt (1 Sam. 18:4). To modernize, that's like giving someone your favorite hunting rifle, fishing pole, knife, and boots. We all need spiritual friends

we can turn to when life gets tough. True friends know us in and out but love us anyway. They love us enough to tell us the truth even when it hurts. True friends build your faith, let you vent without judging, and keep your secrets safe. Later, when Jonathan was slain in battle, David mourned, *"I am distressed for you, my brother Jonathan; you have been very pleasant to me; your love to me was wonderful, surpassing the love of women"* (2 Sam. 1:25-26). It was a different level of love, not romantic or sexual. (Some try to twist this into something perverted. David was not gay; he had multiple wives—2 Sam. 3:2-5.) They shared a deep bond of trust and goodwill that comes from common interests and experiences. It's an "I've-got-your-back-no-matter-what" loyalty that will do anything for a friend in need. Jonathan repeatedly stuck his neck out and helped David avoid King Saul knowing it jeopardized his own chance at the throne. Everyone needs a friend like that they can run to. As Benjamin Franklin noted, "A friend in need is a friend indeed."[24]

3. **David ran to Ahimelech the Priest in Nob** —1 Sam. 21:1-9. Nob was a Levitical city of priests two miles from Jerusalem (1 Sam. 22:19). This was another spiritual place to find sanctuary among godly people. There

David found a priest to console him. We also have a great High Priest we can run to for help (Heb. 4:14-16). He also received provision to sustain him (Ahimelech gave him showbread to feed him and his famished men). Then Ahimelech gave him Goliath's sword. That was a trophy from a former victory which became a prophetic promise. You see, what God has done, He will do again. David's faith must have soared, "If God brought me through the biggest battle of my life, He'll carry me through this one too! The same God who helped me defeat Goliath will deliver me from King Saul." Goliath's sword was a tangible reminder of God's greatness and faithfulness—that caused David to believe, "He will move for me again."

4. **David ran to Gath**—1 Sam. 21:10-15. This was a major mistake. What was he thinking? It was a bad idea to go to Gath, Goliath's hometown, carrying Goliath's sword. That would get you noticed or hurt in a hurry. Achish, King of Gath, means "serpent charmer"[25] (a fitting type of the devil). Gath was a pagan, Philistine city and a hotbed of evil. This is the spiritual equivalent of running to the world and sin for refuge instead of the church. When some people face trouble, they run to drugs, alcohol, immorality,

and other self-destructive addictions. This bad decision led David to fear and foolish behavior. He pretended to be insane (faking a seizure and letting his saliva drool down his beard) in order to escape. Don't run to Gath! The pagan world won't help you. Instead, run to Ramah or Nob, run to God and His people for the help you need.

5. **David ran to the Cave of Adullam**—1 Sam. 22:1-2. David was the original "Captain Caveman." Here we find Captain Dave in his man cave. Adullam means "resting place or hiding place." The Hebrew root means "to dangle" (as a bucket at the end of a rope).[26] David was at the end of his rope. When you get to the end of your rope, tie a knot and hang on! That's usually when God shows up. Exhausted, David hit rock bottom, then God started turning things around. He brought 400 men (diamonds in the rough) into his life for him to lead and mentor. "*Everyone who was in distress … in debt, and … discontented gathered to him. So he became captain over them*" (1 Sam. 22:2). Talk about a rag tag, motley crew of misfits! But God used David to turn these losers into winners and many of them later became mighty men of valor in his army. In our times of brokenness, God teams us with other broken people who are going through

> similar situations. It's mutually beneficial—we need them and they need us.

So, where are you running today? Are you running toward God (to Samuel, Jonathan, or Ahimelech)? Or are you running away from God (to Gath)? Trouble in life is inevitable. Just remember, you have a refuge you can run to—"***God is our refuge*** *and strength, a very present help in trouble*" (Ps. 46:1).

problem situations. He constantly, continually [illegible] we need Him and He needs us.

So where are you running today? Are you running toward God for shelter, comfort, or a hiding place? Or are you running away from God like Jonah? Troubles [illegible] are inevitable, but you have a choice where you run to. God is our refuge and strength, a very present help in trouble (Psalm 46:1).

CHAPTER 7

Faith That Is Unshakeable

In 1957, Jerry Lee Lewis recorded the hit song "Whole Lotta Shakin' Goin' On."[27] Elvis Presley recorded his version of it in 1970. Of course, that secular song referred to shaking bodies on the dance floor as the rock 'n roll craze swept our nation. There's a different kind of shaking happening today—a spiritual, political, economic, and social shaking. While people, governments, institutions, and all sectors of society are being rocked with change and uncertainty, we, the church, must maintain an unshakeable faith that is anchored securely in the Rock of Ages!

The race riots and elections of 2020, the persistent pandemic, interruptions in supply chains, shortages of parts and products, plus a series of natural disasters have shaken our society to the core. Everything, it seems, has changed, from the way we have church, to the protocols kids face in schools, to how we conduct business and meetings, to the way we shop. Not much is "normal" anymore. Pastor Tony Evans said it well, "Don't get shook up when things get shaken up!"

The author of Hebrews prophesied—*"Yet once more I* ***shake*** *not only the earth, but also heaven." Now this, "Yet once more," indicates the removal of those things that are being* ***shaken****, as of things that are made, that* ***the things which cannot be shaken may remain****. Therefore, since we are receiving a kingdom which cannot be shaken, let us have grace, by which we may serve God acceptably with reverence and godly fear"* (Heb. 12:26-28). God is shaking the world and the church in these last days. Everything that can be shaken will be shaken! The good news is we are part of an unshakeable kingdom—*"Upon this rock I will build my church; and the gates of hell shall not prevail against it"* (Mt. 16:18, KJV).

Paul refused to be shaken by his adverse circumstances. Even though he faced persecution, opposition, hardship, hatred, threats, danger, and infirmities, he remained unshakeable! Like water off a duck's back, he just let it all roll off. He said, ***"None of these things move me****, nor do I count my life dear to myself, so that I may finish my race with joy"* (Ac. 20:24). As the old hymn proclaims, "Though the tempest rages, I shall not be moved. On the rock of ages, I shall not be moved ... Though all hell assail me, I shall not be moved, Jesus will not fail me, I shall not be moved, just like the tree that's planted by the water, I shall not be moved!"

Just as a building is only as strong as its foundation, our lives are only as stable and sturdy as our spiritual base. We are either building our lives on solid rock or on sinking sand. Jesus shared this analogy in the Parable of the Two Builders in Luke 6:47-49: *"Whoever comes to Me, and hears My sayings and does them, I will show you whom he is like: He is like a man building a house, who dug deep and laid the foundation on the rock. And when the flood arose, the stream beat vehemently against that house, and* ***could not shake it****, for it was founded on the rock. But he who heard and did nothing is like a man who built a house on the earth without a foundation, against which the stream beat vehemently; and immediately it fell. And the ruin of that house was great."* Notice the storms battered both houses. No matter what we do, the storms of life are coming, you can count on it. After the storms subsided, one house collapsed while the other house was still standing—unshaken!

Jesus is the rock of our salvation. If we build our lives on the rock-solid truth of His Word, we will not be shaken. As another great hymn expresses, "My hope is built on nothing less, than Jesus' blood and righteous; I dare not trust the sweetest frame but wholly lean on Jesus' name … When darkness veils His lovely face, I rest on His unchanging grace; In every high and stormy gale, my anchor holds within the veil. On Christ the solid Rock I stand, all other ground is sinking sand, all other ground is sinking sand!"

Solomon's Temple was destroyed by the Babylonians in 587 B.C. The Prophet Haggai preached after the Babylonian Captivity. About 80,000 captives returned to Israel eager to rebuild their towns, their Temple, and their lives. They quickly became discouraged due to few workers, little money, inferior materials, and King Darius II's order to stop rebuilding the Temple. Then Haggai uttered a powerful prophecy that has already been fulfilled once in history but will happen again in the last days. *"For thus says the Lord of hosts: 'Once more (it is a little while)* ***I will shake heaven and earth, the sea and dry land; and I will shake all nations****, and they shall come to the Desire of All Nations, and I will fill this temple with glory,' says the Lord of hosts … 'The glory of this latter temple shall be greater than the former,' says the Lord of hosts"* (Hag. 2:6-7, 9).

This prophecy was fulfilled over the next few centuries. The Persia Empire fell to Greece, Greece fell to Rome, and the nations were "shaken" in war by these clashing empires. Before and during the time of Christ, Herod spent over forty years remodeling and enlarging the Temple to win political favor with the Jews (Jn. 2:19-21). What made Herod's Temple "greater" than Solomon's Temple? It was larger, fancier, more expensive, and Rome paid the tab. (If it's God's will, it's God's bill!) But what truly made it "greater" was the ONE who visited it! He was dedicated there as an infant, made annual pilgrimages to it for Passover, and taught there during His earthly ministry. In fact, Jesus said, *"A greater than Solomon is here!"* referring to Himself (Mt. 12:42).

Futuristically, the glory of the latter house (the church) will be greater than the glory of the former house again. God likes to save the best for last. The church is not going out with a whimper; it's going out with a roar! God is causing and allowing a "whole lotta shakin' to go on in these last days, but His Word and His true church will be unshakeable! So, don't be shaken by the chaos in the world, the uncertainty of the future, the tragedy of the pandemic, the instability of the economy, attacks of the devil, persecution from unbelievers, sinners acting like sinners, or the liberal policies of our own government. Determine that no matter what happens in the world, in the church, and in your own life, you are going remain USHAKEABLE in your faith! As Paul wrote to the Corinthians, *"Be steadfast, **immovable**, always abounding in the work of the Lord, knowing that your labor is not in vain in the Lord"* (1 Cor. 15:58).

Chapter 8

How Healthy Is Your Heart?

God's main concern is, and our main concern should be, the condition of our heart. It is more important than the condition of our body, our car, our house, our yard, our clothes, or anything else. There are numerous "heart healthy" foods on the market now that are low in sodium, low in fat, low in cholesterol, and low in taste (lol). Many people are health conscious, and rightfully so. If we are mindful about the shape of our physical heart, shouldn't we be equally attentive to our spiritual heart?

Your physical heart is a vital organ (muscle), about the size of a fist, that pumps blood throughout the body. On average, the adult heart beats about seventy-two times per minute—that's 103,680 beats per day,[28] automatically without even thinking about it. God wisely designed our amazing circulatory system (60,000 miles of arteries, veins, and capillaries that would circle the globe two and one-half times at the equator[29]) to ensure that every cell gets its blood supply. The heart is one of our most important organs (when it quits working, we die!). A person can have many other health problems, but if their heart is healthy, they will usually survive.

In a spiritual sense, our heart is the engine of our whole being, the core of who we are. Your "heart" is your true character, nature, attitudes, and motives—the real you on the inside. In Strong's Exhaustive Concordance of the Bible, which is a listing of the primary words contained in the King James version of the Bible, the brain is not mentioned once, whereas the heart is cited in over 900 references. Most of these refer to the spiritual heart not the physical organ. The heart is so important that Scripture tells us to make it a top priority to protect it from negative influences. One key verse is, *"Guard your heart above all else, for it determines the course of your life"* (Pr. 4:23, NLT). You can have many things going wrong in your life, but if your heart is right with God, you can still thrive.

People tend to focus on our looks, personality, possessions, or talent; God focuses on our heart! Remember when God sent Samuel to anoint a new king of Israel? When he saw Jesse's eldest son, Eliab, he was immediately impressed with his muscular physique. He jumped to the conclusion, *"Surely this is the Lord's anointed!"* (1 Sam. 16:6, NLT)

God reminded Samuel that He wasn't looking for the strongest, tallest, smartest, or most handsome man, He was looking for a pure-hearted man of character to wear the crown. *"Do not look at his appearance or at the height of his stature, because I have refused him. For the Lord does not see as man sees; for man looks at the outward appearance, but* ***the Lord looks at the heart****"* (1 Sam. 16:7).

Samuel interviewed all of Jesse's sons (Eliab, Abinadab, Shammah, Nethanel, Raddai, Ozem—1 Sam. 16:6-10, 1 Chr. 2:13-15). The three oldest served as soldiers in King Saul's army and were fine specimens of humanity—strong studs who were tall, dark, and handsome. But none of them were chosen. Frustrated, Samuel asked Jesse, *"Are these all the sons you have?" "There is still the youngest," Jesse replied. "But he's out in the fields watching the sheep and goats." "Send for him at once," Samuel said. "We will not sit down to eat until he arrives"* (1 Sam. 16:11, NLT). David was so young and insignificant he wasn't even invited to the party. He was overlooked by his own father, and by his brothers, and even by the prophet Samuel, but God noticed him. He was a scrawny kid, the runt of the litter, but God saw something different in him—the heart of a champion! God's not looking at your hair, your face, your clothes, your car, your house, your bank account, your intelligence, or your talent; He's looking at your HEART!

The human heart is easily corrupted—*"The heart is deceitful above all things, and desperately wicked; who can know it?"* (Jer. 17:9) The good news is Doctor Jesus still performs heart surgery, even total transplants! *"I will give you a new heart and put a new spirit within you; I will take the heart of stone out of your flesh and give you a heart of flesh"* (Ezk. 36:26). Jesus promised, *"Blessed are the pure in heart, for they shall see God"* (Mt. 5:8). C. S. Lewis observed, "It is safe to tell the pure in heart they shall see God, for only the pure in heart want to."[30] Not only will they see God in heaven, they will see God intervene in their lives here on earth. To be "pure" means "without mixture, or free from anything of a different, inferior, or contaminating kind."[31] A thoroughbred dog has a pure bloodline. Pure gold has no other alloys mixed in with it.

How does God purify our hearts? By placing us in the fire. The most precious metals go through the hottest fires. *"Silver and gold are purified by fire, but* ***God purifies hearts****"* (Pr. 17:3, TLB). When gold and silver are melted down, the impurities rise to the surface. Then, the dross is removed, and the process is repeated. A silversmith knows it is pure when he can look at the liquid silver and see a clear reflection of himself. How long will the purifying process last? Until God can look at us and see a clear reflection of Himself. No wonder Job, who endured many fiery trials, said, *"When he tests me, I will come out as pure as gold"* (Job 23:10, NLT).

The human heart is like wax—close to heat, it softens; away from heat, it hardens. When we are close to God (who is a consuming fire—Heb. 12:29), our hearts stay soft; when we drift away from Him, our hearts harden. Like David, the man after God's own heart (Ac. 13:22), we should constantly pray, "*Create in me a* ***clean heart****, O God; and renew a right spirit within me*" (Ps. 51:10, KJV). Do a self-check-up today; how healthy is your heart? With God, the heart of the matter is always the matter of the heart!

Chapter 9

Attracting God's Attention

We all want God's attention, right? The best way to get His attention is to give Him our full attention and pay close attention to what attracts Him. There are certain attitudes and actions which attract God and others that repel Him. We want to create an atmosphere that is inviting to God's presence.

Hunters attract wild game with certain sights, sounds, and smells using bait and decoys. Sharks are attracted by blood and chum. What attracts romance with our spouse? We spruce up in nice outfits, spray on perfume or cologne, play soft music, and have a candle-light dinner. We create the right atmosphere and set the mood. Likewise, there are at least eight specific things which attract God's attention:

1. **Praise:** Sincere praise is irresistible to God for He *"inhabits the praises of Israel"* (Ps.

22:3). To inhabit means "to live in, dwell in, remain, abide, to sit down as a judge (in a seat of honor)."[32] Paul and Silas were beaten and bound in the Philippian Jail. At midnight, they started singing praises to God who sent an earthquake to shake the prison and *"all the doors were opened and everyone's chains were loosed"* (Ac. 16:26). Notice praise not only opened their prison door; it opened ALL the prison doors! If we learn the secret of getting free in praise, it will not only deliver us but those around us too. (Apparently, Elvis wasn't the first one to sing "Jailhouse Rock!") Hebrews 13:15 reminds us to *"offer **the sacrifice of praise to God continually**, that is, the fruit of our lips giving thanks to His name."* Praise grabs God's attention.

2. **Worship:** The difference between praise and worship is like the difference between chit-chat and a serious conversation. Praise is more *about* God while worship is directly *to* God. Praise tends to be louder, more exuberant, and vocal. Worship tends to be deeper, quieter, and more heartfelt. Praise is like the boisterous waves on top of the ocean; worship is like the strong current deep below the surface. Jesus told the Woman at the Well, *"The hour is coming, and now is, when the true worshipers will*

worship the Father in spirit and truth; for the Father is seeking such to worship Him" (Jn. 4:23). When we sincerely and earnestly worship God, heaven takes notice. It is like a sweet-smelling incense that ascends before His throne. They say the way to a man's heart is through his stomach (think food). Well, the way to God's heart is through the portal of worship.

3. **Prayer:** History proves that God moves when His people pray. Psalms 145:18 declares, "*The Lord is **near** to all who call upon Him, to all who call upon Him in truth.*" Psalms 34:17 adds, "*The righteous **cry out**, and the Lord hears, and delivers them out of all their troubles.*" Israel's desperate cry in Egyptian slavery got God's attention and He raised up Moses to deliver them (Ex. 2:23-25). When Blind Bartimaeus desperately cried out to Jesus, He stopped in His tracks and healed him (Mk. 10:46-52). I'm not talking about a wimpy, mealy-mouthed, half-hearted prayer. Don't expect a $100 answer to a 10-cent prayer! When our kids call us, we might go to them at our convenience; when they cry, we go running to them. You see, it takes more than a need to get God's attention. There are plenty of people in need who don't get a response from heaven. There is a spiritual principle that works—"*Ask and*

you will receive, seek and you will find, knock and the door will be opened to you." Prayer is the key that unlocks the door to all the resources of heaven.

4. **Humility:** Pride is first on the list of things God hates (Pr. 6:16). *"God resists the proud, but gives grace to the humble ... Humble yourselves in the sight of the Lord, and He will lift you up"* (Jam. 4:6, 10). Ahab was the most wicked king in Israel's history (1 Kgs. 21:25). Elijah prophesied that the dogs would lick his blood, devour his wife, Jezebel, and every male in his family would be killed. How did Ahab respond? He tore his clothes, put on sackcloth, fasted, walked meekly, and it captured God's attention. *"See how Ahab has humbled himself before Me? Because he has humbled himself before Me, I will not bring the calamity in his days"* (1 Kgs. 21:29). If God showed mercy and postponed judgment on vile King Ahab because he humbled himself, He will certainly do the same for us.

5. **Repentance:** Genuine repentance—a godly sorrow for sin, hating and forsaking sin—gains God's attention. *"The Lord is near to those who have a broken heart, and saves such as have a contrite spirit"* (Ps. 34:18). Why did God forgive and restore King David when he failed so miserably? Because he

was a true worshipper who humbled himself in real repentance (Ps. 51:9-17). What's true for an individual is also true of a nation—*"If My people who are called by My name will humble themselves, and pray and seek My face, and* ***turn from their wicked ways****, then I will hear from heaven, and will forgive their sin and heal their land"* (2 Chr. 7:14). True repentance is like shooting up a spiritual SOS flare. God notices and rushes to our rescue.

6. **Faith:** God gravitates toward faith while doubt repels Him. The Israelites *"limited the Holy One of Israel"* with their chronic unbelief (Ps. 78:41). Paul warned, *"Whatsoever is not of faith is sin"* (Rom. 14:23, KJV). Unbelief grieves God. Notice how in Nazareth, Jesus' hometown, *"He could do no mighty work there, except that He laid His hands on a few sick people and healed them. And He marveled because of their unbelief"* (Mk. 6:5-6). Faith pleases God (Heb. 11:6) and is a catalyst that releases miracles. God gravitates toward people who walk in faith and believe His Word.

7. **Obedience:** *"**IF** you are willing and obedient, you shall eat the good of the land"* (Is. 1:19). Notice this promise is conditional. God's love is unconditional but His blessings are conditional upon our obedience. Jesus said,

"If you love me, keep My commandments" (Jn. 14:15). Cornelius, a Gentile, Roman Centurion, got God's attention by his kindness and generosity. God even sent Peter, who was biased against Gentiles, to his house where Cornelius' entire family was filled with the Holy Spirit. God told Cornelius, *"Your prayers and charities have not gone unnoticed by God"* (Ac. 10:4, TLB). His obedience attracted God's attention and He poured out spiritual blessings on his whole household.

8. **Unity:** God doesn't bless strife; He blesses unity. What produced Pentecost? About 120 disciples tarried together for 7-10 days in prayer *"with one accord"* (Ac. 2:1). Their unity attracted God's attention and He poured out His Spirit in a phenomenal way. There's power in unity. One can put 1,000 to flight, but two can put 10,000 to flight (Dt. 32:30). David compared unity to the holy anointing oil that was poured on Aaron when he was consecrated as the High Priest and to the refreshing dew that descends on the mountains of Zion where God commanded His blessing (Ps. 133:1-3). Unity attracts God's presence like a heat-seeking missile which explodes with His power and glory.

Imagine being stranded on a deserted island and a plane flies over. What would you do to get the pilot's attention? Would you be casual, calm, and quiet? Or would you run, jump up and down, wave, and yell, "HELP?" Perhaps we need a greater sense of urgency to get God's attention (Ps. 42:1-2). Attracting God's attention is vital because He can do what no other power can do!

Chapter 10

Winning the War Over Worry

An unknown author wrote, "Worry is a futile thing, somewhat like a rocking chair, although it occupies your time, it doesn't get you anywhere."[33] In His famous Sermon on the Mount, Jesus warned all worrywarts with the phrase *"Take no thought"* (KJV) four times. Modern versions render it *"Do not worry."* Worrying seems harmless enough. No big deal, right? After all, everybody worries. John Haggai said, "You could write on countless American gravestones the epitaph: Hurried, Worried, Buried!"[34] Can you relate?

The definition of the word "worry" indicates its nefarious nature—"To torment oneself or to suffer from disturbing, negative thoughts."[35] It comes from an Old English word *wyran* which means, "To strangle, choke, bite, harass, or to tear at the throat with teeth."[36] The imagery is of a predator biting the neck of its prey to suffocate it. The enemy's goal is to drain the spiritual life out of us with stress and anxiety. Holocaust survivor Corrie Ten Boom wrote, "Worry doesn't empty tomorrow of its sorrow; it empties today of its strength."[37] Worry happens when we assume responsibility God never intended for us to have. Peter provided some sound advice, *"Give all your worries and cares to God, for He cares about you"* (1 Pt. 5:7, NLT). God invites us to unload all our heavy burdens on Him. Mary Crowley said, "Every evening I turn my worries over to God. He's going to be up all night anyway!"[38] We should often do what the old hymn suggests, "Take your burden to the Lord and leave it there."

Worry is an issue of faith—do we trust God or not? Worry is a sin because it is a symptom of a lack of trust in God. *"Now if God so clothes the grass of the field, which today is, and tomorrow is thrown into the oven, will He not much more clothe you,* ***O you of little faith****?"* (Mt. 6:30) Mahatma Gandhi said, "There is nothing that wastes the body like worry, and one who has any faith in God should be ashamed to worry about anything whatsoever."[39] If a Hindu had that much insight, when will blood-washed, born-again, Spirit-filled Christians realize that God is in control? Dr. Maxwell Maltz observed, "The greatest cause of ulcers is mountain climbing over molehills."[40]

1. Don't worry about daily provisions.

Centuries before supermarkets, shopping malls, and Amazon, Jesus said, "*Therefore I say to you, **do not worry** about your life, what you will eat or what you will drink; nor about your body, what you will put on ... Look at the birds of the air, for they neither sow nor reap nor gather into barns; yet your heavenly Father feeds them. Are you not of more value than they?*" (Mt. 6:25-26) If God clothes and feeds the natural world, He'll certainly provide for His spiritual family. Even when God feeds the birds, He doesn't throw the food in their nests. Remember, God rained manna from heaven to feed the Israelites, but they still had to gather and prepare it for consumption. Notice, too, that God did not provide a weekly or monthly supply. Instead, He provided a daily supply. Why? So, they would depend on Him every day. The Lord's Prayer petitions, "*Give us this day our **daily** bread.*" Human tendency is to stockpile and hoard, but God wants us to trust Him day by day for supernatural provision.

The word "provision," contains the prefix "pro" meaning "before" and the root word "vision" which means "to see."[41] Put them together and you get "to see before." In other words, Jehovah Jireh—The Lord Our Provider—sees our need in advance and begins to supply it. God placed the ram on Mount Moriah before Abraham arrived and realized he needed a substitute for Isaac. "*And **my God shall supply all your need** according to His riches in* *glory by Christ Jesus"* (Phil. 4:19). Why worry about provision when your heavenly Father is the great Provider?

2. **Don't worry about things you can't control.**

Jesus challenged His listeners, *"Which of you by **worrying** can add one cubit to his stature?"* (Mt. 6:27) Another version reads, "Which of you by worrying can add even one hour to his life?" We spend too much time obsessing and stressing out over things like traffic, weather, gas prices, aging, the stock market, the past, politics, etc. It's counterproductive to worry about things we can't change. Instead, Jesus told us to focus on our chief concern, *"Seek the Kingdom of God above all else, and live righteously, and he will give you everything you need"* (Mt. 6:33, NLT).

3. **Don't worry about the future.**

"Don't be anxious about tomorrow. God will take care of your tomorrow too. Live one day at a time" (Mt. 6:34, TLB). Now, this does not mean that we shouldn't plan or save for the future. If we fail to prepare, we prepare to fail. If we don't pray and plan for the future, we won't have a very good one. It means, "Don't worry about the future, for God is already there!" To quote Corrie Ten Boom again, "Never be afraid to trust an unknown future to a known God."[42] Every tomorrow has two handles—the handle of anxiety or the handle of faith.

Billy Graham observed, "I've read the last page of the Bible. It's all going to turn out right."[43] We can rest in the realization that God's purpose and plan will ultimately be fulfilled. Have you ever wondered why God doesn't reveal our entire future to us all at once? First, it would probably overwhelm us. Secondly, He wants us to walk by faith. We may not know what the future holds, but we don't have to worry because we know Who holds the future!

A modern beatitude reads, "Blessed is the man who is too busy to worry by day and too tired to worry by night."[44] Paul gave us the ultimate weapon to win the war against worry—*"Don't worry about anything; instead, pray about everything"* (Phil. 4:6). Why worry when we can pray?

Chapter 11

Renewing the Altar Experience

An altar is a place where God alters our lives. Altars are mentioned over 400 times in the Bible indicating their prominent role in lives of God's people. Most Old Testament characters built or used them to offer animal sacrifices as atonements for sin and to worship Yahweh—the one, true God. In ancient times, an altar was usually a simple stone structure on which religious rites were performed. Pagans sacrificed at shrines often called "high places" (elevated or hilltop sites) to please and appease their false gods or idols. In Christian churches, an altar is a place to stand or kneel before the Lord to worship or pray. Salvation often occurs on an initial trip to an altar, but the altar should be used regularly thereafter. Done properly, the altar experience brings us and keeps us close to God. An altar is not limited to a fixed location inside a church building; it can be anywhere we contact heaven and make a spiritual connection with our Creator.

The first "altar experience" presumably occurred in the Garden of Eden. Prior to the fall, there was no need for an altar because Adam and Eve enjoyed unbroken fellowship with their Maker (Gen. 3:8). After the fall, God made them coats of animal skins setting a precedent—the only way sinful man can be accepted in the presence of a holy God is with a blood sacrifice (Gen. 3:21). The first parents must have modeled the altar experience or how else would Abel have known how to bring an acceptable sacrifice to God? Cain offered fruits and vegetables he grew and was rejected, while Able brought a lamb (a blood sacrifice) and was accepted. Ironically, the first murder was over religion. In these brothers we see a contrast of two religions: Cain represents the religion of works (man's effort to reach God); Abel represents the religion of grace (God's effort to reach man).

The first altar actually mentioned in Scripture was after the flood, when *"Noah built an **altar** to the Lord, and … offered burnt offerings on the altar. And the Lord smelled a soothing aroma"* (Gen. 8:20-21). God later gave specific instructions on how to make altars (Ex. 20:24-26). He gave these instructions right after He gave the Ten Commandments because he knew man would fail and would need a way to return to God. Abraham built several altars, most notably the one on Mount Moriah which he named *Jehovah-Jireh* because God provided a substitute sacrifice (a ram) for his son Isaac (Gen. 22:9-14). Notice Abraham laid his most precious possession on the altar. God did not take Isaac from him, but He did require that he place him on the altar. Later, Isaac and Jacob built their own altars to the Lord (Gen. 26:25; 35:1). Centuries later Moses built an altar to honor God for helping Israel defeat the Amalekites and called it *Jehovah-Nissi*, meaning "the Lord our banner" of victory (Ex. 17:15). Joshua, Samuel, David, and Solomon all built altars. When God called Gideon to deliver Israel from the Midianites, he named his altar *Jehovah-Shalom*—the Lord our peace—to proclaim how God can provide peace even in a time of war. Furthermore, he destroyed his father's pagan altar earning him the nickname "Jerubbaal," meaning "striver against Baal" (Jgs. 6:24-32).

Both Moses' Tabernacle and Solomon's Temple contained a brazen altar. It was the first article of furniture inside the doorway of the Outer Court. Before the priests could enter the Holy Place, they had to offer atonements (coverings for sin) on the brazen altar and wash in the brazen laver (a basin of water). Brass in Bible symbolism speaks of judgment. So, sin had to be dealt with first before they could approach God's presence. The Tabernacle and Temple also contained a golden altar inside the Holy Place. This altar was only used to burn incense, symbolic of prayer and worship (Rev.

5:8; 8:3-4). It was placed directly in front of the veil (curtain) to the Holy of Holies indicating that prayer and worship is the closest thing to the heart of God and our highest calling. David understood the symbolism, *"Let my prayer be set before You as* ***incense****, the lifting up of my hands as the evening sacrifice"* (Ps. 141:2).

When Elijah confronted King Ahab and the false prophets of Baal on Mount Carmel, he "***repaired the altar*** *of the Lord that was broken down"* (1 Kgs. 18:30). God's altar had been forsaken and replaced with pagan altars to Baal—the storm, rain, and fertility god who was worshipped as "the rider of the clouds."[45] But Baal was powerless to send rain to end the drought or to send fire on the heathen altar. Then Elijah did the unthinkable—he poured twelve barrels of water over the sacrifice on God's altar. Water was the most valuable commodity of that time. Remember, it had not rained for over three years. Crops and livestock were dying, rivers and lakes were drying up, and people were starving from the drought. But an empty altar receives no fire. One man had the courage to repair the broken altar and look at the result: God sent fire from heaven to consume the sacrifice, a backslidden nation repented, rained was restored, and Israel won a total spiritual victory.

The altar has been neglected or replaced in too many lives, homes, and churches. An altar is spiritually significant in many ways and represents a place of sacrifice, judgment, death, repentance, atonement, forgiveness, transfer, prayer, worship, victory, deliverance, and breakthrough. The altar is where we die to our will and surrender to God's will. Animal horns were often placed on the four corners of altars to tie sacrifices down (Ps. 118:27). A horn is an animal's strength, defense, and a powerful weapon against any enemy. Likewise, our source of strength and the key to spiritual victory is found in renewing the altar experience. Like Elijah, let us repair the broken altar and watch God alter our lives and circumstances for our good and for His glory.

PART 2

Inspired Insights on Social Issues

CHAPTER 12

Brainwashed in Babylon

Thousands of Israeli captives were uprooted from their homeland and relocated to Babylon. In ancient times, POWs were often imprisoned or enslaved. King Nebuchadnezzar took the cream of the crop and groomed them to be leaders in his government. They were given a three-year, crash course on Chaldean culture—the language, customs, education, religion, and all the ways of Babylon (Dan. 1:1-5). The goal was to make them to forget their heritage and train them to think, act, talk, look, and live like Babylonians.

Daniel was probably a descendant of King Hezekiah, a Prince of Judah (2 Kgs. 20:17-18), and a eunuch since he never mentioned a wife or children. He and his comrades were in Babylon, but they were not of it—they were Israelites, children of the living God. They were in exile, "a prolonged separation from one's country or home."[46] Babylon is symbolic of the world's system that is controlled by the spirit of the Antichrist. We are also exiled in spiritual Babylon. This world is not our home. We are just pilgrims passing through.

You can trace Babylon's rotten roots back to Nimrod who was a mighty hunter and king (Gen. 10:9-10). Unlike his righteous great grandfather, Noah, Nimrod was rebellious. His name means "let us rebel or he who rules."[47] His kingdom was called Babel in the land of Shinar (where the Tower of Babel and Babylon were later built). Some say he was the first to try to institute a one-world government. Babylon means "confusion" and is a type of this world's fallen, corrupt system that tries to rule without God, resulting in confusion and chaos where there should be order and purpose.

Daniel and his companions lived clean in a corrupt culture. They honored God, refused to worship idols, or be brainwashed in Babylon. They faced a fiery furnace and a den of lions, but God delivered them and promoted them to prominent positions of power. His favor on their lives was unmistakable! They avoided Satan's secret, five-fold agenda for the king's seed:

1. Reprogram your mind:

Nebuchadnezzar tried to retrain their brain so they would forget all about the God of Israel. Public education indoctrinates our kids with evolution, humanism, liberalism, and secularism. Students are taught that abortion, pornography, and pre-marital sex are acceptable, and that homosexuality and transgenderism are normal and desirable. Remember, Babylon means "confusion."[48] There is confusion over what is right and wrong because biblical values are not taught. With a tsunami of secular education and entertainment, is it any wonder why society is unraveling? When people reject God's truth, they are left with man's wisdom which is foolishness. C. S. Lewis noted, "Education without Christian values, as useful as it is, seems to make people more clever devils."[49] The Apostle Paul wrote, *"Professing themselves to be wise, they became fools"* (Rom. 1:22) and *"Ever learning, and never able to come to the knowledge of the truth"* (2 Tim. 3:7). Satan tries to reprogram our minds with deceptive lies; God renews our minds with liberating truth.

2. Replace your diet:

Every day the captives were served gourmet meals from the king's kitchen—Chaldean chow and Babylonian bologna! *"But Daniel was determined not to defile himself by eating the food and wine given to them by the king"* (Dan. 1:8, NLT). The "unclean" food violated Daniel's convictions, so he requested a substitute diet of vegetables and water (what is now commonly called the "Daniel Fast"). What was the big deal? The king's meat was unclean for one of three reasons: 1. The meat was either soaked in blood, raw, or cooked rare, common among the Gentiles but forbidden to Jews

(Lev. 17:11-12). 2. The meat was from an unclean species of animal banned by Mosaic Law and shunned by kosher Jews. 3. The meat was sacrificed to idols. In any event, the food was taboo. We also have a daily choice—we can binge on secular grub (worldly entertainment) or we can feast on spiritual things (the bread and meat of God's Word and the water and wine of the Spirit). We are what we eat physically and spiritually. Why eat out of the devil's dumpster when God has spread a banqueting table before us? Daniel and his friends lived on veggies and water for three years and they were healthier, wiser, and "ten times better" than everyone else (Dan. 1:15-20). What are we feeding our mind and our spirit? Carnal junk food or healthy soul food?

3. Remake your identity:

Notice they were all renamed in Babylon. Their Hebrew names associated them with the one, true God of Israel; their Babylonian names tied them to pagan gods (Dan. 1:6-7). Daniel means "God is my Judge."[50] His Babylonian name, Belteshazzar, means "Bel protects his life" (the patron god of war).[51] Hananiah's name, meaning "Jehovah is gracious,"[52] was changed to Shadrach which means "Commander of Aku" (a moon god).[53] Mishael's name, "Who is like God,"[54] was changed to Meshach, "Who is like Aku."[55] Azariah's name, "Jehovah is my keeper/helper,"[56] became Abednego, "Servant of Nebo" (a god of literature, wisdom, and arts).[57] Despite this effort to remake their identity, the Hebrews never forgot who they were. They were Israelites and princes of the Most High God. Likewise, we must never forget our true identity. By faith in Jesus, we are the children of Abraham (Gal. 3:7, 29), sons and daughters of the living God, heirs of God and joint heirs with Christ (Rom. 8:17).

4. Reproach your testimony:

What if they had compromised and caved in to temptation? There would be no Book of Daniel. If satanic powers can tarnish our character, they can undermine our credibility. When a witness testifies in court, the opposing lawyer tries to trash their credibility so no one will believe them. Daniel lived above reproach. His enemies spied on him and tried to dig up dirt on him to stain his reputation but couldn't find any (Dan. 6:3-4). Imagine a modern politician with no scandal. How refreshing that would be! Daniel is one of a few Bible characters with no flaw on his record. Perhaps he benefitted from writing his own book (autobiographies are kinder to the subject than biographies). Still, the only thing his enemies could accuse him of was that He prayed too much. Wow! What an awesome testimony!

5. Reclaim your worship:

It's all a tug-of-war over worship—God wants your worship and Satan wants your worship. Narcissistic Nebuchadnezzar built a golden image (perhaps of himself) over 100 feet tall. Then he coerced the masses to worship it (Dan. 3:1-5). Shadrach, Meshach, and Abednego (or I should say, Hananiah, Mishael and Azariah), refused to bow down and worship this idol. Consequently, they were thrown into a fiery furnace, but God protected and promoted them. When King Darius was tricked into signing a bogus bill outlawing prayer, Daniel prayed anyway and was thrown into a lion's den, but an angel gave them lockjaw. They thrived in a corrupt culture, served in the highest levels of government, and made a powerful impact for the kingdom of God! Daniel and the three Hebrews never forgot who they were (Israelites not Babylonians), where they were from (the Promised Land, not a pagan empire), and who they worshipped (Jehovah/Yahweh, not the gods of Babylon).

Paul reminded us, *"Don't copy the behavior and customs of this world, but let God transform you into a new person by changing the way you think"* (Rom. 12:2, NLT). Someone said, "The most frequently washed part of the body is the brain." Friend, don't allow yourself to be brainwashed in Babylon!

Chapter 13

Avoiding the Isolation Trap

One of the worst spiritual traps we must avoid is isolation. No person is an island to himself. We were not designed to live in prolonged solitude but to interact in a network of healthy relationships. Isolation is not healthy for us physically, emotionally, mentally, or spiritually. We need meaningful relationships with other people and genuine fellowship with other believers.

Creation itself proves this point. When God surveyed His work after each of the first five days of creation, He saw that, *"It was good."* On the sixth day, after He formed man in His own image, He observed, *"It was VERY good"* (Gen. 1:31). Then, on the seventh day, God rested. Why? Was He tired? No, God paused to appreciate His work and enjoy communion with the man He made.

Adam had God and more pets than a zoo-keeper prior to the fall. Yet God noticed something was missing. God made the first and only negative observation concerning His otherwise perfect creation—"*It is **not good** that man should be **alone**; I will make him a helper comparable to him*" (Gen. 2:18). God realized Adam wouldn't thrive in seclusion, so He made him a companion. God knew man needed help. He couldn't tend the garden, take care of the critters, and produce and raise a family alone. From Adam and Eve's union came the first family, then clans, communities, towns, cities, nations, and a world population that is presently bulging at 7.9 billion people.

One author noted, "Alone and without love we die. Life is as dependent upon relationships as it is on food."[58] A scientist performed an experiment with puppies. He took two dogs of the same breed and fed them the exact same diet. One was placed in solitary confinement; the other was given interaction with people and other dogs. Over time it thrived, but the isolated pup eventually became sick and died. Satan's strategy with people is similar—he wants to drive us into isolation. Why? Because when we're alone, we're much more vulnerable to temptation, fear, depression, and even suicide. Think about it, when did the serpent tempt and deceive Eve? Apparently, when Adam was absent. When did the devil tempt Jesus? When He was alone in the desert and was weak from forty days of fasting.

What happens when you isolate one coal from

the other coals in a fire? The single coal will burn out. When did Elijah suffer his severe bout with depression and battle suicidal thoughts? Not when he was leading the crowd in prayer on Mount Carmel but when he was camping alone in a cave. Jezebel put a bounty on his head and he fled from Jezreel to Beersheba, the southern border of Israel (about 113 miles), then he walked another day's journey (20-24 miles). Then he sat under a juniper tree and prayed to die. He didn't really want to die. If he did, he should have stayed where Jezebel's henchmen could find him. He was discouraged, emotionally drained, physically fatigued, mentally burned out. God sent an angel to minister to him, and feed him, who said, *"the journey is too great for you"* (1 Kgs. 19:2-8). If a mighty prophet like Elijah needed supernatural help, we also need God's help and other people's help. We can't do it all alone. We have an unhealthy tendency to withdraw into a shell and push people away when we need them the most.

When predators like a pack of wolves or a pride of lions hunt, they usually isolate sick or weak prey from their herds. They gang up on one victim instead of attacking a united herd. By instinct they know it's easy pickings. The Bible speaks of the power of partnership, *"If two of you agree on earth concerning anything that they ask, it will be done for them by My Father in heaven"* (Mt. 18:19). The principle is true—one can put 1,000 to flight, two can put 10,000 to flight (Dt. 32:30). There is strength in numbers, *"Five of you shall chase a hundred, and a hundred of you shall put ten thousand to flight; your enemies shall fall by the sword before you"* (Lev. 26:8).

In Ecclesiastes 4:9-12, Solomon shared four benefits of friendship:

1. Increased productivity:

Verse 9—*"Two are better than one, because they have a good reward for their labor."* A team can accomplish much more than any individual. In a horse pulling contest, the 1st place winner pulled 4,500 pounds. The 2nd place winner pulled 4,000 pounds. Hitched together, they pulled 12,000 pounds. That's the power of partnership!

2. A strong support system:

Verse 10—*"For if they fall, one will lift up his companion. But woe to him who is alone when he falls, for he has no one to help him up."* When you are struggling, strong friends will support you and vice versa. Geese flying in a V formation can fly much farther and faster as a unified team than they can individually. When they get tired, they rotate from the front of the formation to the back where less wind resistance makes it easier to fly. The geese in the back honk encouragement to the ones in the front. As John Maxwell says, "Teamwork makes the dream work!"[59]

3. Comfort:

Verse 11—*"Again, if two lie down together, they will keep warm; but how can one be warm alone?"* This world is a cold, cruel place. We draw comfort and warmth from people who provide emotional and spiritual support.

4. Protection:

Verse 12—*"Though one may be overpowered by another, two can withstand him. And a threefold cord is not quickly broken."* Even the Lone Ranger had Tonto to team up and fight with him. We all need people in our corner who have our back. We can't defeat demonic forces by ourselves, we need some tag team partners to help us fight the good fight of faith.

That's why Jesus sent His disciples out two by two (in pairs)—for accountability, to have a witness, for protection, and for moral and spiritual support. Some negative things resulted from two or three years of on and off quarantining during the recent pandemic. Some people spent so much time alone, they fell into depression and despair. People spent way too much time staring at computer, TV, and phone screens. Suicide increased among certain demographics and addictions rose as coping mechanisms.

We are not designed to live in isolation. Don't let the enemy isolate you from friends, family, or the fold. If it wasn't good for Adam to be alone in

Eden paradise, it's certainly not good for us to be alone in a broken world. We need human interaction and frequent fellowship with other believers and with God. No wonder Hebrews 10:25 warns, *"Not forsaking the assembling of ourselves together, as is the manner of some, but exhorting one another, and so much the more as you see the Day approaching."* We can have private, personal devotions at home, but it is a totally different dynamic when we gather together for corporate worship with other believers. Friend, don't allow yourself to become a victim of the isolation trap.

Chapter 14

Faith or Presumption?

With the Coronavirus outbreak in 2020, many Christians wrestled with the balance between faith in God's power over disease and the prudence of social distancing. Certainly, we trust God and believe that He can and will protect us from sickness. The power of Jesus' name is greater than any virus. However, where do we draw the line on taking unnecessary risks? Many pastors grappled with this reality as we temporarily closed our churches and held online services in order to protect our flocks and curtail the pandemic.

Jesus, you recall, dared to touch lepers as He healed them (Mk. 1:40-42). One could argue, "True, but He is God!" Yet He told His followers to do the same, *"And as you go, preach, saying, 'The kingdom of heaven is at hand.' Heal the sick,* ***cleanse the lepers****, raise the dead, cast out demons"*

(Mt. 10:7-8). Jesus also used the spoken word to heal people without laying hands on them (Mt. 8:5-13). I've made many hospital visits where I was required to wear a mask, gown, and gloves to pray for patients with contagious conditions. Admittedly, quarantine is not fun. We don't like our freedoms restricted but, remember, God "quarantined" Noah's family for about a year on the ark for their own safety. God also made the Israelites stay inside their houses as the destroyer passed over Egypt. Yes, they were protected by the blood, but they had to remain inside or risk exposure and death (Ex. 12: 22-23). God had Moses isolate lepers from the camp and burn contaminated clothes to prevent epidemics (Lev. 13:45-59). Rahab's family was also confined to her house when God razed Jericho as the scarlet cord hung in her window as a token of divine protection (Josh. 2:18-19).

Walking by faith is one thing; straying into presumption is another. Notice when Satan tempted Jesus to jump off the top of the Temple, he used Psalms 91:11-12 to bait Him. Christ didn't fall for the trap, *"It is written again, 'You shall not tempt the Lord your God'"* (Mt. 4:5-7). As God in a human body, He could have jumped and landed safely. He was not bound by natural laws. After all, He walked on water, passed through walls, calmed storms, multiplied food, and traveled supernaturally at times. However, He refused to follow Satan's suggestion or to tempt God. To "presume" means "to assume, to take for granted, to undertake with unreasonable boldness, to do something without the right or permission, to go too far in acting or in taking liberties."[60] This means there are some limits to faith that prevent us from being reckless.

Acting with cautious wisdom does not indicate a lack of trust in God. A series of sayings provide perspective: We trust God but we wear seat belts. We trust God but we wash our hands. We trust God but we wear life jackets. We trust God but we use oven mitts with hot dishes. We trust God but we lock our houses at night. We trust God but use smoke detectors in our homes. We trust God but we take medicine and so on.

Consider these biblical examples that illustrate the difference between faith and presumption:

- Faith prompted Noah to build the ark and it succeeded; pride and presumption motivated men to build the Tower of Babel and it failed.
- Israel routed Jericho by faith and obedience; they were humiliated by Ai due to overconfidence and compromise—Josh. 7:1-12.
- Israel placed the Ark of the Covenant ahead of their army and God fought their battles; backslidden Israel later tried it and 36,000 men were slain and the Ark was stolen by the Philistines—Num. 10:33-35, 1 Sam. 4:3-22.

- Barnabas' faith prompted him to sell his land, donate the profit to the church, and he was blessed; Ananias and Sapphira did the same thing deceitfully and they were cursed—Ac. 4:36-37; 5:1-11.
- Faith empowered Paul to cast out demons; the seven sons of Sceva presumed to practice exorcism and they were injured and humiliated—Ac. 19:12-16.

Truth taken to extremes becomes heresy. Some people even take Jesus' words too far, *"And these signs will follow those who believe: in My name … they will take up serpents; and if they drink anything deadly, it will by no means hurt them"* (Mk. 16:17-18). Paul was bitten by a venomous viper on the Island of Melita while building a fire. The superstitious natives assumed he was a murderer and waited for him to drop dead. When he survived, they thought he was a god. Paul wasn't hunting for snakes, but God protected him when he accidentally contacted a deadly one (Ac. 28:1-6). People who handle snakes or drink poison on purpose to prove their "faith" are tempting fate and often suffer fatal results. Besides, Jesus also said, *"Behold, I give you the authority to trample on serpents …"* (Lk. 10:19). Why handle them when we can trample them?

We know God rewards bold, aggressive faith, but He also expects us to use common sense. For instance, we shouldn't grab a live electrical wire, jump out of a plane without a parachute, play in the street, run up big debts and hope for a bailout, or do other foolish, dangerous things and expect divine intervention. God protected the three Hebrews in the fiery furnace, but they didn't jump into the fire voluntarily. Yes, God kept Daniel safe in the lion's den, but he didn't leap into it to prove he had faith.

In 1910, as a plague ravaged Africa, Pentecostal preacher, John G. Lake, experienced a series of verified miracles. The plague was so contagious, they offered $1,000 (big money back then) to nurses who dared to care for the sick. Lake and his team volunteered for free. They entered houses, removed and buried the dead, but no symptoms of the plague touched them. Finally, a doctor asked him, "What have you been doing to protect yourself? You must have a secret." Lake responded, "Brother, it is the law of the Spirit of life in Christ Jesus. I believe that just as long as I keep my soul in contact with the living God so that His Spirit is flowing into my soul and body, that no germ will ever attach itself to me, for the Spirit of God will kill it." Lake invited the doctor to experiment by taking the foam from the mouth of a dead plague victim and put it under a microscope. He saw masses of living germs. Then Lake told the doctor to put the foam on his hands. The doctor did so and watched the germs die instantly in Lake's hands.[61]

So, concerning Covid-19 and other contagious

outbreaks, we know and believe God can, did, and will protect us. In retrospect, we now realize that some of the restrictions imposed during the pandemic were excessive and more about government overreach and control than public safety. For instance, in some states, governors tried to close churches while casinos, night clubs, and other businesses remained open. They threatened to fine churches and arrest the pastors if they tried to hold worship services. They even tried to tell congregants not to sing in churches. Fortunately, many courageous pastors stood up for their religious freedoms and their right to worship and the Supreme Court ruled in their favor. At the same time, some social distancing was a sensible precaution not a lack of faith. Did we dare to minister to those who contracted the virus? Yes. Did we trust God? Certainly! Did we wash our hands and try to stay out of harm's way? Absolutely! May God help us to find the proper balance; to continue to walk in faith yet avoid presumption.

Chapter 15

Bats in the Belfry

It's not unusual for bats to find refuge in a belfry (a bell tower either attached to a church steeple or another structure). In a figurative sense, to have "bats in one's belfry" is an idiom that means to have crazy ideas, to be very peculiar, erratic, or foolish.[62] For example, if you think you can paddle across the ocean in a canoe, you have bats in your belfry—you're nuts.

A few years ago, something strange happened at our house. Our double garage/basement doors were left open one evening. As dusk settled, my oldest son closed the automatic roll up doors, unaware that a bat flew in and was trapped in the basement desperate to escape. Sometime later, my wife and youngest son went downstairs to drive somewhere. Suddenly, I heard a commotion. I jumped up from my office chair and ran toward the loud noise. My wife and son came running back up the stairs yelling, "There's a bat in the basement!" Startled, because bats give me the hee-bie-jeebies, I grabbed a broom and warily descended the stairs. In the basement, I saw the foul fowl fluttering around erratically. He made a few passes and darted toward me Kamikaze style. Quickly, I ran through the basement, opened both big doors, waved the broom wildly, and finally managed to shoo the creepy critter out. I climbed the stairs like a superhero who just rescued my family from a super villain and certain doom and declared, "I am Batman!"

Believe it or not, bats are actually mentioned in the Bible three times. In two instances (Lev. 11:19, Dt. 14:18), they are listed among the unclean birds Israelites were forbidden to eat. Believe me, there is no danger of this Gentile violating that ancient, Jewish, ceremonial law. No bats for me, thank you. In the final reference, Isaiah 2:20 described idols being thrown *"to the moles and bats,"* where abominations belong. So, all three references portray bats in a negative manner. Bats are nocturnal creatures and are often associated with Halloween and horror films. My point is a bat doesn't belong in your house and neither does another spiritual intruder—hatred.

If you claim to be a Christian, hate should have no place in your heart. It is one thing to disagree with people's views or opinions and disapprove of their words or actions, but it is another thing to harbor hatred. We must remember that God hates sin, but He loves sinners. If He didn't, churches and heaven would be empty. Late in life, John the Beloved became known as the "Apostle of Love," but he didn't begin that way. As a young disciple, Jesus gave him and his brother, James, the unflattering nickname "Boanerges," which means "sons of thunder" (Mk. 3:17). In other words, they were hot-headed, quick-tempered, argumentative, and ready spout to off their opinions. Billy Graham said it well, "Hot heads and cold hearts never solved anything."[63]

On one occasion, John informed Jesus, "*Master, we saw someone casting out demons in Your name, and we forbade him because he does not follow with us.*" But Jesus said to him, "*Do not forbid him, for he who is not against us is on our side*" (Lk. 9:49-50). Just because people don't associate with your group doesn't mean they should be vilified as an enemy. Some people are so small-minded that if something is not happening in their church, denomination, or circle of friends, they assume it can't be good or of God. But God is so much bigger than our little religious cliques.

Another time, as Jesus and His disciples approached a Samaritan village, they were turned away. Notice John's irrational overreaction, "*When ... James and John saw this, they said, 'Lord, do You want us to command fire to come down from heaven and consume them, just as Elijah did?' But*

He turned and rebuked them, and said, 'You do not know what manner of spirit you are of. For the Son of Man did not come to destroy men's lives but to save them'" (Lk. 9:54-56). Their prejudice against Samaritans was so deeply inbred that they were ready to burn them all up at the slightest provocation. Jesus rebuked them and told them they had the wrong spirit. Americans and Christians today need to repent for any and all racism, renounce it, and ask God to remove it from our society. Bats don't belong in your basement and bigotry doesn't belong in your heart! David's prayer is especially relevant in our increasingly hostile racial climate, "*Create in me a clean heart, O God; and* ***renew a right spirit within me***" (Ps. 51:10, KJV).

Remarkably, though John grew up with hatred in his heart, after spending time with Jesus and seeing true love (agape) modeled, he was transformed. As Martin Luther King expressed, "Darkness cannot drive out darkness; only light can do that. Hate cannot drive out hate; only love can do that."[64] Later, we read how John returned to Samaria with Peter to assist Philip the Evangelist in a city-wide revival (Ac. 8:12-17), evidence of his changed heart. Instead of praying fire down from heaven to destroy them, he prayed for the fire of the Holy Spirit to empower them. John went on to write most of what the New Testament says about love. In his writings, he used some form of the word "love" over 100 times.

Once consumed by hate, John was transformed into the Apostle of Love. His words still soothe the souls of millions today, *"Beloved, let us love one another, for love is of God; and everyone who loves is born of God and knows God. He who does not love does not know God, for God is love"* (1 Jn. 4:7-8). As MLK admirably said, "I have decided to stick with love. Hate is too great a burden to bear."[65] Now is the time to take a spiritual broom and sweep the bats and the bigotry out of our lives. If you think you can be a true Christian and hold on to hatred, then you, my friend, have bats in your belfry!

Chapter 16

Scandals and Scoundrels

In the past few years, we have seen a tidal wave of sex scandals and shamed scoundrels. Hundreds of prominent men were accused of sexual harassment or misconduct after movie producer Harvey Weinstein's scandal broke in October of 2017, and the "#MeToo" movement swept the country. An epidemic of moral corruption was exposed as big names fell like dominoes. Let me be clear, the guilty should confess, repent, and resign their leadership positions. The rest of us should search our hearts and pray God helps us keep our own noses clean. We, the members of God's church, can't afford to stick our heads in the sand and ignore this issue if we wish to remain culturally relevant. In response, we need to remind ourselves of the biblical boundaries for sexual behavior and how Scripture says women should be viewed and treated.

Sadly, the sexual revolution of the 60s and 70s is still producing rotten fruit. Generations with no moral compass or restraint have sown to the wind and now we are reaping the whirlwind (Ho. 8:7). Many who have sown their wild oats are praying for crop failure, but an inescapable law is set in motion—"*Do not be deceived, God is not mocked; for whatever a man sows, that he will also reap. For he who sows to his flesh will of the flesh reap corruption, but he who sows to the Spirit will of the Spirit reap everlasting life*" (Gal. 6:7-8). Hollywood is partly to blame for this tsunami of immorality. The entertainment industry vomits a steady stream of sexually graphic TV shows and movies that portray women as sex objects. Pornography flows like an open sewer on the internet, and we wonder why sexual assaults and date rape are rampant on college campuses and in society. What do we expect? We, as a nation, have rejected God's Word which provides proper boundaries for sexual conduct. We now live in an "anything goes, if-it-feels-good-do-it" society.

God is certainly not anti-sex. After all, He invented it! Sexuality is a special gift God designed for married couples to enjoy and express their mutual love. But He also established safeguards, not to deprive us of pleasure, but to protect us from disease, premature pregnancy, broken hearts, abuse, guilt, and shame. Which would you prefer, a fence at the top of the cliff or an ambulance at the bottom? God's Word is the fence that prevents us from going over the cliff. While God will forgive and restore anyone who has failed morally if he or she repents, the adage is still true—"An ounce of prevention is worth a pound of cure." God is a master at restoration, but He prefers prevention and can keep us from falling in the first place if we cooperate with His Spirit (Ju. 1:24). It's good to have a safety net; it's better not to need one.

The Bible is crystal clear about sexual behavior—*"Marriage is honorable among all, and the bed undefiled; but fornicators and adulterers God will judge"* (Heb. 13:4). *"For this is the will of God, your sanctification: that you should* ***abstain from sexual immorality****"* (1 Th. 4:3-4). It is inappropriate to touch anyone in a sexual way except your legal spouse. Though our sick society says otherwise, adultery, fornication, incest, homosexuality, rape, prostitution, pornography, and pedophilia are all still forbidden (Lev. 18:6-26; 19:29, Dt. 22:25, Mt. 5:27-28, Eph. 5:3). Sex, like a fireplace, is a wonderful benefit to enjoy in its proper setting, but if the flames get outside the hearth, they will burn your house down.

There's an intriguing account of sexual harassment in Genesis, but it's opposite of the usual way. Instead of a man pushing for sex, it was a woman. Potiphar's sensual wife held all the cards in this scenario. (While men have taken most of the hits in the media lately, reports abound of male and female leaders alike who abuse their positions and seduce their subordinates.) After Potiphar promoted Joseph from a slave to the steward of his household, his wife *"began to look at him lustfully. 'Come and sleep with me,' she demanded"* (Gen. 39:7, NLT). Genesis 39:10 indicates that this was not a one-time occasion, but she tried to entice Joseph daily. When he repeatedly rebuffed her advances, she falsely accused him of attempted rape and had him arrested. Later, God exonerated him and exalted him from the prison to the palace due to his integrity. Joseph never compromised even in the face of torrid temptation; a lesson for us all.

The key word the Bible uses regarding the treatment of women is "honor." The Hebrew word *kabad* translated "honor" means "to be heavy" or "to make weighty,"[66] because valuable things tend to be heavy such as gold, silver, and precious stones. So, to honor others is to treat them as valuable, to give weight to their words, and to cherish them as the true treasure they are. How do you treat a costly crystal vase? You treat it carefully as something precious that has special worth. The Ten Commandments, the teachings of Jesus, and the writings of Paul all exhort us, *"**Honor** your father and mother."* Peter instructed husbands to live *"with understanding, **giving honor to the wife**, as to the weaker vessel, and as being heirs together of the grace of life"* (1 Pt. 3:7). Paul directed husbands to *"love your wives, just as Christ also loved the church and gave Himself* *for her*" (Eph. 5:25). Paul also told Timothy, to treat "*older women as mothers, younger as sisters, **with all purity***" (1 Tim. 5:2).

In many countries women are battered, abused, mistreated as inferior, and kept in strict submission. They are deprived of education, not allowed to vote, drive a car, work outside the home, or leave their house without permission. If they disobey their husbands, they are punished. Oppressing women is evil and contrary to Scripture. In the biblical model, God made men and women equal yet unique. When God formed Eve, He didn't use Adam's foot bone which might imply inferiority or a skull bone to suggest superiority. Rather, God used a rib which speaks of equality, close to his side and near his heart, so he would love her, and under his arm, so he would protect her. The Bible elevates women to an honored status and teaches to treat them with the highest dignity and respect. To physically, emotionally, sexually, or verbally abuse a woman is an offense against God in whose image she is made. It's time for another sexual revolution in America—a revolt against a culture of corruption and disrespect toward women matched by a renewed passion for purity in ALL our relationships.

Chapter 17

How Jesus Responded to Racism

Jesus went out of His way to break down racial barriers. The racism He confronted was between Jews, Samaritans, and Gentiles. There was even a racial rivalry among the Jews (Judeans derided Galileans and Galileans disdained Nazarenes). This is evident by how Nathaniel stereotyped Jesus, *"Can anything good come out of **Nazareth**?"* (Jn. 1:46) He prejudged Jesus before he even met him based on his bias against Nazarenes.

Racism boils down to PRIDE—the ugly self-deception that "WE are better than THEM." Racism assumes that different means wrong. Remember, we are all made from dirt, plus our bodies consist of about 60% water (dirt + water = Mud!). Paul wrote, *"We have this treasure in earthen vessels"* (2 Cor. 4:7). It not the container that is so valuable to God, but the contents He has placed in it. The ground is level at the cross. We are all equally loved by God and equally in need of His grace. Hatred has no place in the heart of any Christian. God's view on race can be summarized in a simple song most of us learned in Sunday School: "Jesus loves the little children, ALL the children of the world, red and yellow, black and white, they are precious in His sight, Jesus loves the little children of the world!" To be precious means "very valuable, dear, beloved, important, cherished, treasured, prized, priceless."[67]

Jesus dealt with racism among His own disciples and rebuked them for it. As mentioned earlier, James and John, at first, were hate-filled, cold-hearted, hot-headed troublemakers. Jesus even gave them a negative nickname—"Boanerges," which means "sons of thunder" (Mk. 3:17). Thunder makes a lot of noise. These brothers were loud, opinionated, argumentative, and full of hot air. On one occasion, they were angry that some Samaritans turned Christ away from their village and wanted to call fire down from heaven to burn them up. *"But He turned and rebuked them, and said, '**You do not know what manner of spirit you are of**. For the Son of Man did not come to destroy men's lives but to save them'"* (Lk. 9:55-56). If we harbor hatred in our hearts and want to hurt or kill people, we have the wrong spirit. That is not the Spirit of Christ; it's the spirit of Antichrist.

After seeing true love modeled by Jesus, the disciples radically changed. Later, Peter and John returned to Samaria to pray for them to receive the Holy Spirit in Acts 8:12-17. Instead of praying the fire of judgment down on them to curse them, they prayed the fire of the Holy Spirit down to bless them. Once consumed with hate, John later became known as "the Apostle of Love." In fact, in his writings he used some form of the word "love" over 100 times. His words still soothe the souls of millions today—*"Beloved, let us love one another, for love is of God; and everyone who loves is born of God and knows God. He who does not love does not know God, for God is love"* (1 Jn. 4:7-8). We need a fresh baptism of love in our society. If we harbor bigotry, we must repent of it, renounce it, and ask God to remove it from our hearts.

Jesus broke down the barriers between Jews and Gentiles (Eph. 2:11-19). The Gospel is inclusive not exclusive (Jn. 3:16; 12:32, Rev. 22:17). Heaven will be integrated not segregated (Rev. 5:9). Paul preached that we are all ONE in Christ—there is neither Jew nor Gentile, male nor female, black nor white, bond or free (Gal. 3:28). Racial barriers all fall at the foot of the cross and the color line is washed away in the blood of Jesus! Notice How Jesus broke down racial barriers:

- **Jesus went to Samaria to save the Woman at the Well**—Jn. 4:4-9.

Most Jews went the long way around Samaria just to avoid "those people." There was total segregation between Jews and Samaritans in Bible times, and they even worshipped in separate temples (Jn. 4:9, 20). But Jesus had a divine appointment with a broken woman who desperately needed His help. The disciples were shocked that Jesus even spoke to her (Jn. 4:27), yet, He took the time to reveal His Messiahship to her (Jn. 4:25-26). She was a five-time divorcee with a live-in lover, then she met the seventh man—the one she'd been looking for all along. (The number seven indicates completion or perfection in Scripture since God completed creation in seven days and a full week consists of seven days). As a result of Jesus' encounter with the Woman at the Well, a two-day revival broke out in Samaria (Jn. 4:39-42).

- **Jesus healed a Roman Centurion's servant**—Mt. 8:5-13.

We tend to skim over this story without realizing the racial tension between Jews and Romans. The Jews despised them for occupying their land, controlling their lives, and overtaxing their incomes. Jesus was willing to go to the Centurion's house. To us, that's no big deal, but most Jews then wouldn't even consider going near the house of an "unclean" Gentile. The Centurion said Jesus could just speak the word only. He knew how the chain of command worked (his boss gave him orders and he gave his soldiers orders). Then Jesus complimented his faith and healed his servant.

- **Jesus delivered the Syrophoenician woman's daughter**—Mt. 15:21-28.

Jesus ventured beyond the borders of Israel to meet this Greek lady (Mk. 7:26). At first, He ignored her—*"He answered her not a word"* (Mt. 15:23). Then, He excluded her—*"I was not sent except to the lost sheep of the house of Israel"* (Mt. 15:24). Next, it seems, He insulted her—*"It is not good to take the children's bread and throw it to the little dogs"* (Mt 15:26). (Jews often referred to "unclean" Gentiles as dogs.) She must have been a bulldog because she refused to take no for an answer, *"Yes, Lord, yet even the little dogs eat the crumbs which fall from their masters' table"* (Mt. 15:27). Jesus tested her but was so impressed by her faith that He delivered her daughter from demons. The fact that Jesus took the time to minister to this woman proves how He came to break down racial barriers and include the Gentiles who had previously been excluded.

- **Jesus healed a Samaritan leper**—Lk. 17:11-19.

When Jesus cleansed the ten lepers near Samaria, only one returned to give thanks. Luke, the only Gentile Bible author, identified him as a Samaritan. Jesus was amazed, *"Were there not ten cleansed? But where are the nine? Were there not any found who returned to give glory to God* ***except this foreigner****?"* (Lk 17:17-18) Nine Jewish lepers were healed, the grateful Samaritan was made completely whole.

- **Jesus told the Parable of the Good Samaritan**—Lk. 10:30-37.

Samaritans were the "bad guys" to the Jews, but Jesus deliberately made a Samaritan the hero of His story to show there is good in people we may not like. Notice the priest and the Levite (two "good guys") did nothing to help the victim. Jesus redefined who our neighbor is—not just someone who lives on the same street, but any person of any race who is in need at any given time or place.

Jesus included the Gentiles and removed racial barriers. It caused a backlash from His own people and eventually led to His crucifixion. After all, He wasn't just the King of the Jews, as the Samaritans testified, *"We know that this is indeed the Christ, the **Savior of the WORLD**"* (Jn. 4:42). In God's eyes, there is only one race—the human race!

Chapter 18

Why Violence Is Not the Solution

Like many Americans, I was appalled by, and ashamed of, what transpired in Washington D.C. on January 6, 2021, as protesters stormed the capitol. It was an ugly and sad day for America and a bad look to the rest of the world. I love our country deeply and it grieves me to see the hatred and division on both sides. I have no issue with peaceful protesting. I believe the media is often biased and distorts the truth. Plus, in politics people often play dirty (all is fair in love and war and politics).

Some sources say the peaceful protest was hijacked by extremists. Even so, when people cross the line and resort to violence, we condemn it on both sides. While we can't control what's going on in D.C., we can control what's in our own hearts.

We should constantly pray, *"Create in me a clean heart, O God; and* ***renew a right spirit*** *within me"* (Ps. 51:10, KJV). In other words, when the world goes wrong, don't go wrong with it!

Like millions of conservatives, I have questions about the fairness and accuracy of the 2020 election. If there was fraud or corruption, I pray it is exposed. But two wrongs never make a right. Besides, our hope is not in a man or in a political party—our hope is in Jesus! Our future and salvation do not depend on who is in the white house but on who is on the throne! "On Christ the solid rock I stand, all other ground is sinking sand!"

Violence is not the solution because it only breeds more violence in a vicious cycle of revenge. Paul provided the answer—*"Repay no one evil for evil ... If it is possible, as much as depends on you, live peaceably with all men. Beloved, do not avenge yourselves, but rather give place to wrath; for it is written, 'Vengeance is Mine, I will repay,' says the Lord ... Do not be overcome by evil, but* ***overcome evil with good****"* (Rom. 12:17-21).

We are in a spiritual war for the soul of our nation. This unique fortress of freedom is in turmoil (racially, politically, culturally, and, most of all, spiritually). There is a constant clash between good and evil, God and Satan, truth and error, light and darkness, the spirit and the flesh. People are not the enemy but the spirits that work through people.

Paul provided insight into this unseen realm, *"For we wrestle not against flesh and blood, but against principalities, against powers, against the rulers of the darkness of this world, against spiritual wickedness in high places"* (Eph. 6:12).

A major difference between the Old and New Testaments is this: Israel fought mostly natural battles against natural enemies using natural weapons while we are fighting spiritual battles against spiritual enemies using spiritual weapons. We can't win spiritual battles with natural weapons (they tried it in D.C., and it backfired). *"For the weapons of our warfare are not carnal but mighty in God for pulling down strongholds"* (2 Cor. 10:4). We can't defeat the devil or evil with swords, knives, guns, or bombs; we defeat them with the Word of God, faith, prayer, and the name and blood of Jesus.

Jesus dealt with violent tendencies among His own disciples. One of His hand-picked recruits was Simon "the Zealot" which tells us about his political affiliation. The Zealots were a radical, Jewish sect of Zionists who hated Roman occupation and often resorted to violence to incite riots and tried to overthrow Roman rule.[68] Other infamous Zealots were Judas of Galilee who was crucified in a revolt around 6 A.D. (Ac. 5:37), Barabbas (Mk. 15:7), and probably the two thieves crucified with Christ. So, think about it, Jesus chose Matthew (a tax collector) and Simon (an extremist who hated tax collectors) to be on His ministry team. Imagine the arguments they had at the dinner table. There were serious clashes of opinions and, who knows, maybe a few fights.

So, why did Jesus choose a Zealot to be His disciple? Jesus probably had to take him aside a few times and tone him down: *Simon, I know you don't like these people and want to hurt them, but I love them and came to save them. So, mind your manners!* Jesus redirected Simon's political fervor to a greater cause—spreading the Gospel. Jesus replaced his racism and hatred with a genuine love for people. Church tradition says that Simon later preached in Africa, Egypt, and Britain and he was either crucified or sawn asunder for his faith and testimony. Ironically, the disciple who was the most likely to take lives ended up giving his life as a martyr. Christ changed his heart, and a potential murderer turned into a powerful minister. That's what God's grace can do!

Remember, James and John, whom Jesus nicknamed "sons of thunder," also had a violent streak. When a Samaritan village rejected them, they asked for permission to pray fire down from heaven like Elijah did to burn them up. Jesus rebuked them and told them they had the wrong spirit (Lk. 9:55-56). Many people today have the wrong spirit, too—even Christians. People we might dislike or wish harm to are the same people Jesus loves and seeks to save.

When Peter drew his sword to defend Jesus in Gethsemane, He scolded him and healed the man he injured—*"Put your sword in its place, for all who take the sword will perish by the sword. Or do you think that I cannot now pray to My Father, and He will provide Me with more than twelve legions of angels?"* (Mt. 26:52-53) Jesus could have summoned an angelic army to route the Romans and deliver the Jews. Later, He stood before Pilate who demanded, *"Are You the King of the Jews? ... Jesus answered, My kingdom is not of this world.* ***If My kingdom were of this world, My servants would fight****"* (Jn. 18:33, 36). Jesus didn't rally His followers to fight. Instead, He inspired them to change the world with love.

Are there times when violence is justified? Certainly. If someone is being attacked, you have the right to protect them. If someone breaks in your home, you have a right to stand your ground and defend yourself. If you are a soldier in combat for a just cause, not all killing is murder. Somebody had to stop Hitler's Nazism. Somebody had to defeat fascism and communism. Somebody must stop dictators who are hell bent on genocide. Someone must stop violent criminals determined to commit mass murder. Often the only way to stop violent people is with deadly force.

As Christians, we must balance this with the fact that Jesus called us to be peacemakers. When Jesus said, *"From the days of John the Baptist until now* ***the kingdom of heaven suffers violence****, and the violent take it by force*" (Mt. 11:12), He wasn't advocating violence against other people. He was talking about being forceful in a spiritual sense and resisting sin, Satan, self, and the world to press into and promote the kingdom of God (Lk. 16:16).

Yes, we oppose abortion, but we don't harm doctors who perform them or bomb abortion clinics. We disagree with communism, socialism, atheism, and racism, but we don't threaten or physically harm those who embrace these false ideologies (unless they attack our nation or foreign representatives, of course). We disagree with adultery, homosexuality, drugs, drunkenness, and gambling, but we don't hurt people who practice these things. Like Jesus, we love the sinner and loathe the sin. Christ calls us to be peacemakers, not troublemakers. Violence is never the solution. In an increasingly violent world, Paul's message is more relevant than ever, *"Be not overcome with evil but overcome evil with good!"*

PART 3

Inspired Insights on Jesus' Ministry

Chapter 19

The Shepherd and Sheep Analogy

You can read Psalms 23 in about thirty seconds. David's masterpiece is only six verses long, yet it contains a treasure trove of spiritual truth. Sadly, we usually only hear it read at funerals or quoted as a crutch in a crisis. Many Scriptures allude to the shepherd/sheep analogy to describe God's relationship with His people. Prominent shepherds in the Bible include Abel, Abraham, Isaac, Jacob, Jacob's twelve sons, Laban, Moses, Jethro, and David. Oh, and there's one more we can't forget—JESUS! *"The good shepherd gives His life for the sheep ... I am the good shepherd; and I know My sheep, and am known by My own"* (Jn. 10:11, 14).

Psalms 23 starts with the personal name of God, *"The LORD is my Shepherd."* Notice LORD is in all capital letters. In Hebrew, it's *YHWH* (yeh-ho-vaw'). In English, we say Jehovah or Yahweh.[69] This is rendered LORD thousands of times in the Old Testament. Some Jews believed the name of God was too sacred to be spoken, so they put it in a form that couldn't be pronounced. They wrote it like this YHWH (this forms the tetragrammaton or the name of "four letters"). Jehovah or Yahweh means "the self-existent, eternal One."[70] It implies a personal God who dwells among His people and is ready to intervene for them.

There's a big difference between a lord and a savior. Most people want a savior to rescue them from hell (fire insurance), but few want a lord to change their lifestyle. A lord is "a person who has authority, control, or power over others, a master, chief, or ruler." Many people resist yielding control of their will to Christ; they want to be saved and keep doing their own thing. However, if the Lord is truly our Shepherd, then we must yield to His Lordship to stay under the canopy of His blessing and favor.

So again, a primary name for God in Hebrew appears in the beginning of Psalm 23—*Jehovah/Yahweh-Rohi*—the Lord my Shepherd. By nature, sheep are helpless creatures. They are totally reliant on a shepherd to lead them to clean water, green pastures, and protect them from predators. They don't have claws or fangs to defend themselves, plus they run slowly and clumsily. Sheep are mentioned more frequently in the Bible than any other animal (about 750 times)[71] and provide the perfect analogy of how much we need God. *"We are His people and the sheep of His pasture"* (Ps. 100:3). Consider seven benefits we, as sheep, receive from our heavenly Shepherd:

1. **Provision**—*"I shall not want"* (lack).

This implies another name of God—Jehovah-Jireh—the Lord my Provider (Gen. 22:14). He won't finance all our wants, but He did promise to supply all our needs. *"My God shall supply all your need according to His riches in glory by Christ Jesus"* (Phil. 4:19). He is a God of vision and provision who uses supernatural ways and unexpected sources to meet our needs. If it's God's will, it's God's bill!

2. **Direction**—*"He leads me beside the still waters ... He leads me in paths of righteousness."*

Sheep must be led, or they will wander into trouble, fall off a cliff, or eat poisonous plants. Sheep need to drink from still waters. Swift currents are dangerous because, when their fleece absorbs water, sheep become top heavy and can capsize and drown. God gives us clear direction—*"The steps of a good man are ordered by the Lord"* (Ps. 37:23). Plus, the Holy Spirit is our navigator who guides us into all truth (Jn. 16:13).

3. **Restoration**—*"He restores my soul."*

The Hebrew word translated "restores" here is *shub* (pronounced shoob). It means "to turn back, to retreat, withdraw, refresh, or recover."[72] The Message renders it, *"He lets me catch my breath."* We are not designed to go wide open and full speed all the time. Sometimes, we need to step back, rest, and be refreshed in His presence. *"Even though our outward man is perishing, yet the inward man is being* ***renewed*** *day by day"* (2 Cor. 4:16). Restoration results from spending quality time with the Shepherd.

4. **Protection**—*"I will fear no evil: for You are with me."*

This describes a hedge of divine protection. Psalm 5:12 declares, *"For You, O Lord, will bless the righteous; with favor You will surround him as with a shield."* A shield is a protective barrier between you and the enemy. Jesus declared, *"I am the door"* (Jn. 10:9). In Bible times, a sheepfold was often just a simple stone enclosure with an opening for a door. At night, after every sheep was counted, the shepherd laid down in the opening and served as a human gate. No wolf could get in without attacking him first and no sheep could get out unless it climbed over him. Jesus is our Shepherd/Door who keeps us safely in His fold.

5. **Correction**—*"Your rod and Your staff they comfort me."*

The shepherd's staff was a walking stick with

a crook that was used to retrieve wayward lambs. *"All we like sheep have gone astray; we have turned, every one, to his own way"* (Is. 53:6). The rod was a club used to fend off predators. If a sheep strayed habitually, the club might be used to break its leg for its own good. Too many dangers lurk outside the safety of the flock. Then the shepherd would carry that sheep and nurse it back to health. A problem in the modern church and in society is few people get correction without also getting offended. Correction is an unpleasant but vital part of spiritual growth (Heb. 12:5-11). Like surgery, God's discipline is short-term pain in exchange for long-term gain.

6. **Prevention**—*"You anoint my head with oil."*

Ancient shepherds anointed sheep's heads with oil for two reasons: 1. to prevent sunburn or sunstroke (as a simple sunscreen) 2. to prevent disease-causing parasites (as a primitive pesticide). The oil ran into the crevices around the sheep's ears, eyes, and nose to repel flies, fleas, and other harmful parasites that could make it sick and even die. The Holy Spirit's anointing oil keeps us from being scorched by the heat of tribulation and repels negative and demonic influences that try to attack us. No wonder the Psalmist wrote, *"I have been anointed with fresh oil"* (Ps. 92:10).

7. **Abundance**—*"My cup runs over."*

If we stay close to the Shepherd, He will bless us

abundantly! *"Do not fear,* ***little flock****, for it is your Father's good pleasure to give you the kingdom"* (Lk. 12:32). The kingdom contains all that God is and all that God has. Remember, we are heirs of God and joint-heirs with Christ (Rom. 8:17). He is El Shaddai—"the all-sufficient One." He's not the God of barely enough; He's the God who is more than enough! *"No good thing will He withhold from those who walk uprightly"* (Ps. 84:11). The Shepherd can turn your shortage into a surplus overnight.

So, take time to re-read the twenty-third Psalm and listen to the Shepherd speak to you for Jesus said, *"My sheep hear My voice"* and *"He calls his own sheep by name"* (Jn. 10:27, 3).

Chapter 20

Jesus—The Horn of Our Salvation

Horns are very significant and symbolic in Scripture and are mentioned over 100 times. Zacharias, John the Baptist's father, referred to Christ as the "horn of salvation" in his inspired benediction (Lk. 1:69). This is a name or title that God the Father shares with God the Son—"*The Lord is my rock and my fortress and my deliverer … My shield and the* ***horn of my salvation***" (Ps. 18:2). Let's explore what this analogy means.

Horns were used as containers in Bible times. A hollowed-out, animal horn could be used like a canteen or flask to hold liquids such as water, wine, or oil.[73] Jesus, as the horn of our salvation, contains the water of life, the wine of the Spirit, and the anointing oil to pour into our lives. Horns were often used to dispense anointing oil for priests, prophets, and kings. God told Samuel to fill his horn with oil and to anoint David the new king over Israel (1 Sam. 16:1, 13). Later, Zadok the priest anointed Solomon king over Israel in this same fashion (1 Kgs. 1:39). Perhaps the Psalmist had this in mind when he penned, *"But my horn You have exalted like a wild ox; I have been anointed with fresh oil"* (Ps. 92:10).

David alluded to this practice in his famous shepherd Psalm—*"You anoint my head with oil"* (Ps. 23:5). As mentioned in the previous chapter, ancient shepherds anointed sheep's heads for two main reasons: 1. to prevent sunburn or sunstroke (as a simple sunscreen) 2. to prevent disease-causing parasites (as a primitive pesticide). The Greek word *Christ* and the Hebrew word Messiah both mean "the anointed One." So, Jesus, the horn of our salvation, contains the anointing power of the Holy Spirit which He pours into our lives as needed to help us thrive in life and ministry (Ac. 10:38). The anointing helps prevent spiritual burnout in the heat of tribulation and repels spiritual parasites which try to hinder and harm us.

Horns were frequently used as trumpets in Bible times. A musical instrument was created by cutting off the tip of the horn and blowing through it. The curved horns of rams or oxen served this purpose well. These horns, called *shofars* in Hebrew,[74] were blown for several reasons:

- **To call Israel together for a general assembly or to worship:**

Like church or school bells, the horn blast meant something important was about to happen or it was time to travel and move camp (Num. 10:1-3). Trumpets indicated God's visitation on Mt. Sinai (Ex. 19:18-19) and announced sabbath days, feast days, or holy days were beginning. Horns were blown during the offering of burnt sacrifices as a memorial to the Lord (Num. 10:10). The year of Jubilee, also called the Feast of Trumpets, was announced with the blowing of trumpets or ram's horns (Lev. 25:9). The Feast of Trumpets happens every year on the first day of the seventh month—also known as Rosh Hashana (the head of the year). On the tenth day of the seventh month in the year of Jubilee there is also a special blasting of the trumpets.

Christ, as the horn of our salvation, calls us to worship and prayer, motivates us to move forward, and inspires us to seek after God and spiritual things. He puts the desire in our hearts to draw close to God and to pursue His will (Phil. 2:13). As wind blows through a horn to make musical sounds so His breath flowing through us creates worship that echoes back to Him.

- **To alert or warn people of danger:**

Like tornado sirens or amber alerts on our smartphones, watchmen on the walls of ancient cities blew horns to alarm inhabitants that an enemy was approaching or some other danger was threatening. The prophet Joel used this analogy, *"Blow the trumpet in Zion, and sound an alarm in My holy mountain! Let all the inhabitants of the land tremble; for the day of the Lord is coming"* (Jl. 2:1). In the Book of Revelation, trumpets are sounded to indicate the judgment of God is being released on earth (Rev. 8:2, 6). As the horn of our salvation, Christ warns us, sends us alerts, makes us feel uneasy at times, and puts a check in our spirit when something is not right. Be sensitive to His alarm in your spirit.

- **To rally troops for battle:**

A different sound on the horns indicated it was time to charge after the enemy (Num. 10:9). *"The Spirit of the Lord came upon Gideon, and **he blew a trumpet*** [Heb. *shopar*]; *and Abiezer was gathered after him"* (Jdgs. 6:34). When the Israelites marched around Jericho, the priests blew trumpets and, as they shouted, God smashed the massive walls like toothpicks. Even so, Christ, our great High Priest, issues a clarion call for us to fight the good fight of faith against demonic forces and to conquer evil in His name (Rom. 12:21, Eph. 6:12).

- **To celebrate good news:**

The coronation of a new king was announced with horns along with other celebrations (2 Kgs. 9:13). A victorious trumpet will announce the Second Coming of Christ, the King of Kings (1 Th. 4:16). As Barbara Johnson's book title suggests, *"Gabriel's Gonna Toot and We're Gonna Scoot!"*

Both the Brazen Altar and the Altar of Incense in Moses' Tabernacle and in Solomon's Temple had horns on the four corners. Slain animals were tied to the horns of the altar so they wouldn't wiggle themselves free during sacrifice—*"Bind the sacrifice with cords to the **horns of the altar**"* (Ps. 118:27). Christ keeps us consecrated as a living sacrifice on His altar (Rom. 12:1). Just as an animal's power is released through its horns, so our spiritual power comes through prayer at the proverbial horns of the altar. The Altar of Incense was the tallest piece of furniture in the Tabernacle and its horns were sprinkled with blood indicating that Christ is our atonement, and that prayer and worship are our highest callings (Ex. 30:10, Ps. 141:2, Rev. 5:8; 8:3-4). The horns of the altar were also a place of refuge or asylum. Both Adonijah and Joab were temporarily spared from execution when they clung to them (1 Kgs. 1:50-53; 2:28). This speaks of how Christ is our refuge in whom we find safety and sanctuary (Pr. 18:10).

Horns are symbolic of strength and power. Animals with horns or antlers use them for defense. If attacked, they use their horns to protect themselves from predators. Horns speak of the spiritual power to resist and conquer an enemy. Horns also represent the dominion of kings, nations, and empires in the prophecies of Daniel (Dan. 7:24). As the horn of our salvation, Christ, our King, is our strength, our defender, and the source of our power and authority to defeat the devil (Lk. 10:19, Jam. 4:7). Horns are not just used for defense; horns are also weapons to use on offense. We don't just react to what the enemy does against us; we can go on the attack in Jesus' name and reclaim what is rightfully ours (2 Cor. 10:4-5).

In summary, Christ is a dispenser of the anointing oil who calls us to worship and warns us of danger. He is the source and the sound of our victory. He is our defender and the spiritual weapon who fights and wins our battles. He is our sovereign Savior who delivers us from the penalty, power, and presence of sin and grants us eternal life. No wonder He is called "the horn of our salvation."

Chapter 21

The Parable of the Prowler

My wife and I were working at her father's house on September 1st, 2016, when suddenly my phone vibrated in my pocket. Our neighbor called to inform me that our home security alarm had been triggered. So, I sped to our house to find an intruder had tried to kick in the front door (a dirty shoe print was visible, the deadbolt was bent, and the door frame was damaged). Unsuccessful, he went around to our French doors in the back and kicked them in. The alarm squealed and spooked the burglar. As he fled, he slammed his vehicle into our basketball goal, knocking the backboard and rim off the pole. (Part of me hopes it landed on his trunk or tailgate to match the certain dent in his bumper.) Remarkably, nothing was missing from our house. I often pray that angels will surround and protect our home and, if anyone comes on our property with ill intent, the fear of

God will fall on them. Prayers answered!

Scripture compares Satan to a prowler, *"Be on the alert. Your adversary, the devil,* ***prowls around*** *like a roaring lion, seeking someone to devour"* (1 Pt. 5:8, NASB). Jesus warned us of a thief lurking about to steal our spiritual valuables—*"The* ***thief*** *comes only to steal and kill and destroy"* (Jn. 10:10). Satan wants to steal everything valuable in your life—such as your peace, joy, victory, salvation, purity, family, marriage, health, finances. In this same passage, Jesus revealed that He is the "Good Shepherd" and "the door" to the sheepfold. Ancient sheepfolds consisted of a simple stone enclosure with only a rough opening for a door. During the day sheep were led out to graze in the pasture, then at night they returned to the fold. Once they were all accounted for, the shepherd would lie down and sleep in the doorway of the fold. The shepherd literally served as the door. No sheep could get out and no predator could get in unless it climbed over him. No wonder Jesus added, *"My sheep listen to my voice ... I give them eternal life, and they shall never perish; no one will snatch them out of my hand"* (Jn. 10:27-28, NIV). Our protective Shepherd fends off the prowling wolves.

Jesus knew something about thieves. After all, Judas, His treasurer, had sticky fingers (Jn. 12:6). Matthew was a tax collector before becoming a disciple (publicans were infamous for cheating people out of their hard-earned money). Furthermore,

Jesus used robbers to illustrate His sermons. In His "Parable of the Sower," He described how birds (representing the wicked one) swoop in to steal the seed of the Word that is sown in people's hearts (Mt. 13:4, 19). His story of "The Good Samaritan" features a man who was assaulted by thieves and left half dead—a fitting image of all who are victimized by Satan and sin and need to be rescued by the Savior (Lk. 10:30-36). Barabbas, the man whose place Jesus took on the cross, was a notorious criminal whose rap sheet included robbery, murder, and sedition. Finally, Jesus was crucified between two thieves, representing how all humanity has stolen from God's glory.

The crooks at the Temple enraged Jesus the most. Up to four million annual pilgrims flocked to Jerusalem to celebrate the Passover Feast.[75] Each person or family was required to offer a sacrifice. Traveling with homegrown animals was difficult, plus, if the priests found any blemishes, they were deemed unclean or unworthy. Thus, many people bought lambs or doves at the Temple at inflated prices. Another requirement for Jewish males twenty years old and up was the half-shekel Temple tax (Ex. 30:12-16). Roman coins were considered "unclean" and were banned from the Temple site because they bore Caesar's profile, a violation of the 2nd Commandment about graven images. Money changers exploited the exchange rates to make bigger profits.[76] Jesus' objection was not the selling of sacrificial animals or the necessary changing of money, it was the price gouging, the blatant fleecing of God's people. It had degenerated into a money-making scam. Avarice and dead religious ceremony replaced the sincere worship of God. Furious that people were being ripped off, Jesus wove a whip and drove the greedy merchants from the Temple, shouting, *"My house shall be called the house of prayer; but ye have made it a* ***den of thieves****"* (Mt. 21:13). Thieves are lurking near our temples today as well—carnal thoughts, worldly attitudes, selfish motives, and evil spirits that try to steal our passion and priority for spiritual things. We, like Jesus, should use the whip of God's Word to cleanse our own personal temples.

The Second Coming of Christ is compared to a "thief in the night" five times in the New Testament. Jesus said, *"Therefore keep watch, because you do not know on what day your Lord will come. But understand this: if the owner of the house had known at what time of night the* ***thief*** *was coming, he would have kept watch and would not have let his house be broken into. So you also must be ready, because the Son of Man will come at an hour when you do not expect him"* (Mt. 24:42-44, NIV).

Paul reminded us, *"For you know very well that the day of the Lord will come like a* ***thief in the night****"* (1 Th. 5:2). Peter also used this thief in the night analogy (2 Pt. 3:10). How does a thief come? Suddenly, unexpectedly—without warning.

A thief doesn't call in advance and say, "Get your gun ready, I'm coming to steal your stuff tonight at ten o'clock." Twice in the Book of Revelation (3:3; 16:15) Jesus warned He will come like a thief, so we should live in a constant state of readiness for His return and not be caught off guard or unprepared.

Paul shared this insight, *"But you, brothers and sisters, are not in darkness so that this day should surprise you like a **thief**"* (1 Th. 5:4, NIV). In other words, the coming of Christ will shock the world because they will not be ready for it, but the true church will not be surprised because the Holy Spirit is preparing us. Neighborhood Watch stresses vigilance and reporting prowlers in communities, but it's even more important to be watchful for Christ's soon return. Jesus reminded us to stay alert, *"What I say to you, I say to everyone: '**Watch!**'"* (Mk. 13:37, NIV)

So, let's be on the lookout out for prowlers and watch even more for the promise of His coming.

Chapter 22

Fickle Followers

Some of the same people who flocked to Jesus' signs later fled from His sayings. "*A huge crowd followed him, attracted by the miracles they had seen him do among the sick*" (Jn. 6:2, MSG). The same crowd which was convinced of Jesus' Messiahship and wanted to crown Him king deserted Him a day or two later (Jn. 6:14-15, 66). This was in the aftermath of His feeding of the 5,000 men, not counting women and children, the only miracle of Christ recorded in all four Gospels. Riding a brief wave of popularity, Jesus did not cater to the crowd, but rather withdrew from them. Unlike many modern preachers and politicians, Jesus was never swayed by the opinions of the masses, knowing they could change instantly. Remember, some of the same people who waved palm fronds and sang "Hosanna to the King, blessed is He who comes in the name of the Lord," later screamed, "Give us Barabbas" and "Crucify Him" to Pontius Pilate. People's emotions and opinions fluctuate like the stock market. Human nature is fickle—"likely to change, not constant or loyal in affection."[77]

John 6 describes a horde of fickle followers who trailed Jesus because of the loaves He gave them instead of their sense of love for Him or faith in His identity as the Son of God. Jesus bluntly stated, "*The truth of the matter is that you want to be with me because I fed you, not because you believe in me*" (Jn. 6:26, TLB). Who wouldn't follow a Messiah who works miracles and gives away free food? Don't misunderstand, God can and will provide for our physical needs and there are many fringe benefits of serving Him, but He wants to give us more than natural things; He wants to give us spiritual things. Jesus was born in Bethlehem, which fittingly means "house of bread,"[78] and He is the Bread of Life that nourishes the spiritual needs of starving humanity. "*And Jesus said to them, 'I am the bread of life. He who comes to Me shall never hunger, and he who believes in Me shall never thirst*'" (Jn. 6:35). A clever church sign read, "Without the Bread of Life, you're toast!"

The crowd feasted on free bread and fish but found Jesus' strange sayings too hard to swallow. Truth, like medicine, doesn't always taste good or make us feel good initially, but eventually, heals our heart and frees us from falsehood. The statements that offended and provoked the crowd the most were, *"Unless you eat the flesh of the Son of Man and drink His blood, you have no life in you. Whoever eats My flesh and drinks My blood has eternal life ... For My flesh is food indeed, and My blood is drink indeed"* (Jn. 6:53-55). Missing the spiritual truth, they assumed Jesus was speaking literally, *"The Jews therefore quarreled among themselves, saying, 'How can this Man give us His flesh to eat?'"* (Jn. 6:52) They thought this same man they were ready to proclaim the Messiah and crown king had lost His marbles. Jesus was speaking figuratively, not advocating cannibalism or vampirism. To eat His flesh is to partake of His Word, for He is the "Word made flesh" (Jn. 1:14). To drink His blood is to sip in His life-giving Spirit (life is in the blood—Lev. 17:11).

The confused crowd quickly turned into an angry mob. *"On hearing it, many of his disciples said, 'This is a hard teaching. Who can accept it?'"* (Jn. 6:60, NIV) As a result, many of His fickle followers defected from their faith—*"At this point many of his disciples turned away and deserted him"* (Jn. 6:66, NLT). After the massive crowd, who watched Him feed them miraculously, dwindled to a handful, Jesus turned to His trusted twelve and asked, *"Do you also want to go away?"* (Jn. 6:67) Peter responded with keen spiritual insight and a bold affirmation of faith, *"Lord, to whom shall we go? You have the words of eternal life. Also we have come to believe and know that You are the Christ, the Son of the living God"* (Jn. 6:68-69).

So, what is our main motive for following Christ? Is it because of the blessings He bestows on us or because of who He is and how much He deserves our love and loyalty? If God never does another thing for us, He's already done enough for us to serve Him the rest of our lives. We owe an eternal debt of gratitude we can never repay. Repeatedly, the Bible urges us to seek God's face, not just His hand. Seeking His face is pursuing a deep relationship with Him; seeking His hand is merely chasing after the blessings He provides. If we learn to seek His face, His hand of favor will certainly follow. Are we following for the loaves or for the love? Are we merely flocking after His signs or feasting on His sayings? Are we, like spoiled kids who only want money, toys, and candy, seeking after the gifts of God but not the heart of the Giver?

Many fickle followers today are wavering in their commitment and defecting from their faith. Paul warned of a great "falling away" in the last days (2 Th. 2:3) and Jesus predicted widespread apostasy, *"Sin will be rampant everywhere, and the love of many will grow cold"* (Mt. 24:12, NLT). We must determine now more than ever to follow Jesus no matter what. As the old song says, "I have decided to follow Jesus … no turning back, no turning back!" *"Let us hold fast the profession of our faith* ***without wavering****; (for he is faithful that* *promised)*" (Heb. 10:23, KJV). Let's not be like the fair-weather friends who ran after Jesus for miracles and free food, but rejected His words. Let's follow Him for the love not just for the loaves—and refuse to be fickle followers.

Chapter 23

Was Jesus a 'Feel Good' Preacher?

We live in an age of "feel goodism" in a super-sensitive society in which people are offended by any perceived slight. Politically correct police patrol the air waves and red flag certain buzzwords and label those who use them as bigots, racists, sexists, and extremists. Freedom of speech is under attack, especially religious speech, which is often tagged as "hate speech" by secularists who reject biblical truth. Paul warned Timothy, *"For a time is coming when people will no longer listen to sound and wholesome teaching. They will follow their own desires and will look for teachers who will tell them whatever their itching ears want to hear. They will reject the truth and chase after myths"* (2 Tim. 4:3-4, NLT).

Contrary to some opinions, Jesus wasn't always

a Mr. Nice Guy who never offended anyone with His words and always avoided controversy. Some people have the misguided notion that Jesus was a "feel good" preacher who was always sweet, kind, diplomatic, and never made waves or rocked the boat. Are you kidding me? What Bible have they been reading?

Jesus offended many people with unvarnished truth that made them feel uncomfortable (Jn. 6:60-61). The late Jammie Buckingham expressed this reality in his clever book title, *The Truth Will Set You Free, But First It Will Make You Miserable.*[79] Sometimes the truth hurts; it hits us right between the eyes and cuts like a knife. Jesus didn't preach what I call "cotton candy sermons," the type that are in vogue today—fluffy strings of sugar-coated thoughts woven together to make people feel good but containing little spiritual substance. In fact, Mark 13:37 indicates that "*the common people heard Him gladly,*" probably because He told the truth without any religious pretenses or pulling any punches. But make no mistake, not everyone heard Jesus gladly.

I'm not suggesting Jesus intentionally offended people, but the truth He spoke had a way of separating the wheat from the chaff, the sheep from the goats. To be clear, Jesus was loving, graceful, compassionate, and tender-hearted toward the outcasts and downtrodden of society. In fact, He went out of His way to visit where others refused to go. Most

Jews, due to prejudice, traveled around Samaria. Jesus deliberately went through it and broke down cultural and racial barriers by even speaking to "The Woman at the Well" (Jn. 4:4-9). Some things He did were considered scandalous in His culture—touching and healing lepers, befriending publicans and sinners, allowing a "sinful" woman to touch and anoint Him (Lk. 7:36-39), healing on the Sabbath day, and so on. He worked outside the lines of social norms for a Jewish man, especially a rabbi.

Even His own cousin, John the Baptist, didn't fully understand Him. He sent messengers asking, *"Are You the Coming One, or do we look for another?"* (Mt. 11:3) Jesus responded by telling how people were being healed and receiving the Gospel, but then added this tagline, *"Blessed is he who is not* ***offended*** *because of Me"* (Mt. 11:6). Apparently, John was offended by Jesus. Why? He was suffering in prison while Jesus was socializing at dinner parties with sinners. Jesus' style and methods didn't fit the mold of what John expected in a Messiah.

Sad to say, Jesus would not be welcome in many modern churches. He challenged the status quo, ruffled feathers, made enemies, and attacked the religious establishment. Jesus showed compassion to sinners, but He also confronted their sin (Jn. 4:18; 8:11). He was very critical of corrupt religious leaders and even called people by some rather unflattering names:

- He called Herod Antipas, who killed his brother, Philip, and stole his wife, Herodias, a "fox" (Lk. 13:32). Foxes are predators who prey on weaker animals, so Jesus was calling Herod out on his abuse of power.
- Jesus nicknamed James and John "Boanerges" meaning "sons of thunder" (Mk. 3:17), which was not a compliment, but a dig at their loud-mouthed, hot-headed, quick-tempered, prejudiced ways (Lk. 9:49-56).
- He called Peter "Satan" for trying to interfere with God's plan for Him to go to the cross (Mt. 16:21-23).
- He called Judas Iscariot a "devil" and the "son of perdition" for his treachery (Jn. 6:70; 17:12).
- He called His own disciples "doubters" with little faith when He calmed a storm (Mt. 8:26), a "faithless and perverse generation" when they failed to cast out a demon (Mt. 17:17), and "fools" and "slow of heart to believe" when they doubted His resurrection (Lk. 24:25).
- Jesus reserved His strongest verbal barbs for the self-righteous religious leaders. In Matthew 23, He called the Scribes, Pharisees, and Sadducees "blind," "blind guides," "serpents," "a generation of vipers," "fools," and "hypocrites."

Jesus' blunt words didn't always make His hearers feel warm and fuzzy, but, as the old saying goes, "If the shoe fits, wear it." Truth is like medicine; it doesn't always taste good initially, but it will help heal you eventually. Jesus' strange sayings are sometimes hard to swallow, but they are words of life and salvation. Any skilled surgeon will hurt you first in the process of healing you. Jesus' sermons were often surgical—short-term pain in exchange for long-term gain. He performed spiritual surgery on people's hearts with the sharp scalpel of His words.

Some thought Jesus was "mean" when he "put out" the mocking mourners before He raised Jairus' daughter from the dead (Mk. 5:40-41). Others thought He was too extreme when He wove a whip and drove the greedy moneychangers from the Temple (Jn. 2:15). Remember, He's both the Lion and the Lamb—the perfect balance of the tough and tender sides of love. In an age when preachers walk on eggshells to avoid saying anything negative or offensive, the Good Shepherd feeds His sheep what they need, not just what they want to hear. The truth won't always make us feel good, but it will make us free. So, let's keep speaking the truth in love and let the chips fall where they may.

CHAPTER 24

Why Jesus Preached in Parables

Jesus was a master storyteller. He communicated clearly by using many stories, analogies, and metaphors. Parables have been used since ancient times to convey truth in a memorable way. While Jesus didn't invent the parabolic method of teaching, He perfected it. Herbert Lockyer wrote, "In the entire realm of literature there is no book so rich in its parabolic and allegoric material as the Bible."[80]

The words "parable" and "parables" combined appear 47 times in the Gospels (KJV). They come from a Greek word *parabole* (pronounced par-ab-ol-ay') meaning, "a similitude, a symbolic, fictitious narrative of common life conveying a moral, an adage, or a proverb."[81] "The Greek word for 'parable' literally means 'a laying by the side of' or 'a casting alongside,' thus 'a comparison of likeness.' In a parable, something is placed alongside something else in order that one may throw light on the other. A familiar custom or incident is used to illustrate some truth less familiar."[82] So, a parable is:

- A comparison of two seemingly dissimilar objects.
- A short, simple story of common life that conveys a moral lesson or spiritual truth.
- An earthly story with a heavenly meaning.
- "An extended metaphor or simile using figurative language in the form of a story to illustrate a particular truth."[83]

Parables illustrate the invisible (spiritual) world by using analogies from the visible (natural) world. Scholars differ on the exact number of parables Jesus told. We do know He used over 100 metaphors and told at least 36 actual parables—15 are found in Matthew, 6 occur in Mark (4 are repeats), 35 appear in Luke (16 are repeats, 19 are unique), and John recorded many metaphors but no parables. Why Jesus preached in parables:

1. **To fulfill prophecy:**

"All these things Jesus spoke to the multitude in parables; and without a parable He did not speak to them, that it might be fulfilled which was spoken by the prophet, saying: 'I will open My mouth in parables; I will utter things kept secret from the foundation of the world'" (Mt. 13:34-35). One thousand years before Jesus came, the Psalmist Asaph

predicted He would preach in parables (Ps. 78:2-3). Jesus fulfilled every prophecy about His life, ministry, death, burial, and resurrection, including this one.

2. To reveal truth:

"And the disciples came and said to Him, 'Why do You speak to them in parables?' He answered and said to them, 'Because it has been given to you to know the mysteries of the kingdom of heaven, but to them it has not been given'" (Mt. 13:10-11). The mysteries of the kingdom are contained in the parables of the kingdom. Eleven parables in Matthew open with the phrase "the kingdom of heaven is like" or "like unto." Jesus' parables contain profound truths (secrets hidden from the foundation of the world). Parables open our eyes to deeper insights into Christ and His kingdom and give us a greater glimpse into the spiritual realm.

3. To conceal truth:

This sounds contradictory to the previous point, but it is not. Jesus explained, *"Therefore I speak to them in parables, because seeing they do not see, and hearing they do not hear, nor do they understand. And in them the prophecy of Isaiah is fulfilled, which says: 'Hearing you will hear and shall not understand, and seeing you will see and not perceive'"* (Mt. 13:13-14). Not everyone was intended to understand Christ's message. He skillfully used parables to throw curve balls and confuse those who were not open to His message. Like the four types of soil in the Parable of the Sower (wayside, stony, thorny, good ground) some people's hearts were not receptive to the seed of His words. "Parables have a unique way of withdrawing the light from those who love darkness. They have an element of mystery, forcing the listener to meditate on them to fully fathom their meaning. The casual listener is left baffled, hearing the superficial story but failing to grasp the underlying truths conveyed."[84] Carnal minds can't comprehend spiritual things (1 Cor. 2:14). Most of all, to truly understand Jesus' parables, a person must have the influence of the Spirit of truth who reveals "the deep things of God" (1 Cor. 2:10).

4. **To illustrate truth:**

Parables provide examples of how truth applies to everyday life. When a lawyer asked Jesus, "Who is my neighbor?" He responded with the Parable of the Good Samaritan (Lk. 10:29-36). In it, Jesus redefined the term "neighbor" as any person of any race who is in need, not just a person who lives nearby, and He showed how good neighbors treat others. To illustrate the need for persistence in prayer, Jesus shared the Parable of the Unjust Judge (Lk. 18:1-8). His point? If persistence pays with a crooked judge who has no interest in your case, how much more will the just Judge (God) respond compassionately because He has a supreme interest in your case.

5. To make truth relevant and practical:

Around 25% of the Bible is comprised of precepts, laws, and raw truths. The other 75% consists of stories of real people that demonstrate how truth applies to real-life, every-day situations. The stories in the Bible have been preserved for our instruction and inspiration (1 Cor. 10:11). The reason *"the common people heard* [Jesus] *gladly"* (Mk. 12:37) was He brought complex, spiritual truth down to their level by using terms they could easily relate to. He spoke their lingo when he compared God's kingdom to farming, fishing, cooking, shepherding, and agriculture.

6. To captivate people's attention:

Jesus avoided dry, dull sermons on the nuances of the law. Instead, He told interesting stories that captured people's attention and stirred their imagination. People were *"astonished at His teaching, for He taught them as one having authority, and not as the scribes"* (Mk. 1:22). When the Pharisees sent soldiers to arrest Him, they returned emptyhanded and said, *"No man ever spoke like this Man!"* (Jn. 7:46) Jesus conveyed His message in a way that fascinated His followers and confounded His critics.

7. To enable His audience to retain His message:

It's much easier to remember a story than facts, data, and boring information. Statistics show that people only remember about 10-20% of what they hear, but about 30-40% of what they hear and see. Parables create mental pictures that help us retain their message. Jesus' parables are still with us 2,000 years later because people were able to recall and record them in detail for our benefit. Great sermons are not the ones with the most information, but the ones people can remember months or years later. Abraham Lincoln's Gettysburg Address was so short (2-3 minutes) the photographer didn't have time to set his camera up to take a picture,[85] but millions of school kids have memorized his speech. A famous orator, Edward Everett, also spoke that day for two hours but few know anything he said. It's not how long you talk; it's how much you say! Jesus spoke volumes with few words.

8. To expose His enemies' wrong motives:

In the Parable of the Prodigal Son (Lu. 15:1-3, 25-32), Jesus included the "older brother" as a direct rebuke to the Pharisees for their "holier-than-thou" attitude toward sinners. He used the Parable of Lazarus and the Rich Man (Lu. 16:14-15, 19-31) to expose their greed and apathy for the poor. Jesus told the Parable of the Pharisee and the Publican (Lu. 18:9-14) to confront the self-righteous and to prove a repentant heart is better than a religious show. In the Parable of the Wicked Husbandman (Mk. 12:1-12), Jesus expressed how the religious elite rejected God's messengers and even God's own Son.

Everyone loves a good story, right? Well, take some time to re-read Christ's stories and discover their hidden treasures. Kingdom mysteries are buried in the King's parables, and He wants to reveal them to YOU! So, grab a Bible and start digging.

Chapter 25

The Man on the Middle Cross

A wooden plaque my wife bought me sits on a bookshelf in my office. It contains a concise, powerful message—"The man on the middle cross told me I can come." You may wonder what the violent death of a first century carpenter has to do with you. The answer is everything!

Two condemned criminals were crucified on either side of Christ. They hung in naked shame and agony on cruel crosses. They were as guilty as sin and deserved death and hell. At first, they both blasphemed Jesus along with the murderous mob gathered at Golgotha (Mt. 27:38-44). Then something happened. One thief had a dramatic turn of heart. What changed his mind? Perhaps it was seeing the grace with which Jesus suffered and hearing Him forgive His own executioners—*"Father, forgive them, for they do not know what they do"* (Lk. 23:34).

The cursing crook was so moved by Christ's compassion, it ignited faith in his heart that he could be saved too. He offered a simple, sincere, nine-word prayer that changed his eternal destiny, "*Lord, remember me when You come into Your kingdom*" (Lk. 23:42). Max Lucado observed, "The only thing more absurd than his request was the fact that it was granted. He who deserved hell got heaven."[86] What made him think he belonged in paradise? That thief, though crucified on earth for his crimes, walks a free man in heaven because of the man on the middle cross. Jesus promised him, "*Assuredly, I say to you, today you will be with Me in Paradise*" (Lk. 23:43).

What Jesus said to that redeemed robber is a message of hope for us all. If Jesus forgave and saved a desperate, dying thief, He will forgive and save us too. If He promised paradise to a prisoner, He will restore and reward us too. Paradise is a place of future happiness, like the Garden of Eden, a place we also call heaven. None of us deserve this realm of incomparable celestial glory, but the good news is the man on the middle cross said we can come (Jn. 3:16).

You see, the man on the middle cross was no mere mortal. He's the REAL Superman—the Godman (Jn. 1:1, 14, 1 Tim. 3:16). He is Emmanuel—"God with us" (Mt. 1:23). After He calmed a raging storm, His astounded disciples asked, "*What kind of man is this, that even the winds and the sea obey Him?"* (Mt. 8:27, NASB) He was more than a man. I hate to spoil the illusion, but the superheroes we see in movies are fiction. Their "superpowers" are merely movie magic, trick photography, stunt doubles, costumes and makeup, CGI, and special effects. They make it look incredibly real, but it's all fake. Jesus' power is real! He can save lost souls, heal broken bodies, restore wounded hearts, deliver drug addicts, walk on water, and raise the dead.

Most superhero movies share a similar plot—the classic struggle between good and evil. Superheroes save the planet from the threats of super villains. Jesus already did that 2,000 years ago. His name in Hebrew is *Yeshua* and it means "Jehovah/Yahweh is salvation." Jesus—the real superhero—saved us from sin, crushed the serpent, Satan, and conquered death, hell, and the grave. Most heroes wear a cape; our hero wore a cross. He arose victoriously and declared, *"I am He who lives, and was dead, and behold, I am alive forevermore. Amen. And I have the keys of Hades and of Death"* (Rev. 1:18).

The man on the middle cross was our scapegoat. On the Day of Atonement (Yom Kippur) the high priest would lay his hands on a goat and confess the corporate sins of Israel (Lev. 16:21). The term "scapegoat" comes from the Hebrew word Azazel which means "the goat of departure."[87] Symbolically, the sins of Israel were removed as the goat was released to wander in the wilderness. A double transfer occurred—the sins of Israel were transferred to the goat and the innocence of the goat was transferred to them. *"As far as the east is from the west, so far has he removed our transgressions from us"* (Ps. 103:12). In a similar way, Jesus became our substitute at Calvary, *"He was wounded for our transgressions, He was bruised for our iniquities: the chastisement of our peace was upon Him, and by His stripes we are healed"* (Is. 53:5). A song says it well, "I should have been crucified, I should have suffered and died. I should have hung on the cross in disgrace, but Jesus, God's Son, took my place."

The man on the middle cross paid our sin debt. Jesus' death was the payment for every sin that has ever been or ever will be committed (2 Cor. 5:21, 1 Pt. 2:24, 1 Jn. 2:1-2). When He cried, "It is finished," He used the Greek word *tetelestai* which means "Paid in full." Archeologists have found tax receipts on papyrus paper with *tetelestai* stamped on them to indicate a zero balance.[88] As another song says, "He paid a debt He did not owe; I owed a debt I could not pay, I needed someone to wash my sins away, and now I sing a brand, new song, 'Amazing Grace,' Christ Jesus paid the debt I could never pay."

There are two sinister lies people believe that prevent them from being saved. Lie #1 is unrighteousness—"I'm too bad." They assume the vile sins of their past exclude them, but there is no sin too big or too bad for the blood of Jesus to blot out (1 Jn. 1:7, 9). No one is beyond His reach (Is. 59:1, Heb. 7:25). Lie #2 is self-righteousness—"I'm good enough." If we were good enough, Jesus would not have had to die on the cross. *"There is none righteous, no, not one"* (Rom. 3:10). *"For all have sinned and fall short of the glory of God"* (Rom. 3:23). *"All our righteous acts are like filthy rags"* (Is. 64:6, NIV), thus the reason we need a Savior (Eph. 2:8-9).

So, if the devil demands a reason why you should be allowed into heaven, if people wonder how you obtained salvation, if your own mind questions why you have a seat at God's table and a ticket to paradise, your answer is simple, "The man on the middle cross told me I can come." If we, like the redeemed robber, repent and believe, we belong in paradise. *"The Spirit and the Bride say, 'Come.' Let anyone who hears this say, 'Come.' Let anyone who is thirsty come. Let anyone who desires drink freely from the water of life"* (Rev. 22:17, NLT).

Three men, three crosses, one hill.

One man cursed, one man prayed,
one man promised.

One died condemned, one died forgiven,
one died innocent.

One died in sin, one died to sin,
one died for sin.

One was held by death, one was released by
death, one conquered death.

One lost life, one gained life, one was life.

—Author unknown

Chapter 26

A Fake Snake on a Stake

Every story in Scripture teaches us either what to do or what not to do, sometimes both. These history lessons were recorded so we can glean wisdom from them. Why fall into the same trap they fell into? Why not avoid their mistakes? The ancient account of the venomous vipers infesting Israel's camp is mentioned five times in Scripture by four different authors (Num. 21:4-9, Dt. 8:15, 2 Kgs. 18:4, Jn. 3:14, 1 Cor. 10:9) adding weight to its importance and credibility.

Paul explained why these stories are still relevant to us, *"Now these things became our examples, to the intent that we should not ... tempt Christ, as some of them also tempted, and were destroyed by serpents ... Now all these things happened to them as examples, and they were written for our admonition"* (1 Cor. 10:6, 9-11).

Israel had just come through a tough time of

national mourning. Both Miriam and Aaron died a few months apart in the previous chapter so they were at a very low place emotionally (Num. 20:1, 22-29). Once again, they couldn't find water in the wilderness. When God used Moses to miraculously bring water out of a rock, they were happy temporarily (Num. 20:8-11). Plus, the king of Edom denied them passage through his land, so they had to take the long route around (Num. 20:14-21). Then they won a battle against the king of Arad's army (Num. 21:1-3). They were on a roller coaster ride of ups and downs, highs and lows. Sound familiar? Don't be a Yo-Yo Christian—up and down, flying high one day, then dragging bottom the next. Our emotions will fluctuate, but our devotion must remain constant.

"*And the soul of the people became very **discouraged** on the way*" (Num. 21:4). Discouragement is one of the biggest tools in the devil's bag of dirty tricks. To discourage means "to deprive of courage, hope, or confidence, to dishearten, dissuade, or to cause to lose enthusiasm."[89] We all battle discouragement when we feel like we're on a spiritual treadmill and not making progress. When the future seems hopeless, we start feeling helpless. Remember, as Bill Bright said, "With God life is an endless hope. Without God, life is a hopeless end!"[90] Keep fighting the good fight of faith. Press on and pray through negative thoughts and emotions. Surround yourself with positive friends. Feed your faith and starve your doubts. Sometimes it's the last key on the ring that opens the lock. So, keep asking, seeking, and knocking because eventually you will receive a breakthrough.

Israel used their same old playbook when they faced problems: 1. Complain, 2. Talk favorably about Egypt, 3. Blame Moses. They fondly remembered the plentiful food of Egypt, but conveniently forgot the downside (slavery). When we speak negativity and unbelief, we open the door to demonic influences—"*For whatsoever is not of faith is sin*" (Rom. 14:23, KJV). The snakes crawled into the camp on the heels of their complaining.

- **The Crisis:**

God sent fiery serpents (poisonous snakes) to chasten His people. Like a scene in a horror movie, snakes bit people, victims convulsed in pain, and slowly died in agony. Chaos ensued as people ran, screamed, and killed snakes with shovels and sticks. Imagine the panic when these slithery critters crawled in people's tents. Numerous graves were dug, bodies were buried, and funerals were held. Serpents are symbolic of demons and venom represents the poison of sin with which we've all been infected (Rom. 3:23; 6:23). The people begged Moses to pray for God to "take away" the serpents. Notice God didn't remove them immediately, but He did provide a way of salvation.

- **The Cure:**

God told Moses to "*Make a fiery serpent and set it on a pole; and it shall be that everyone who is bitten, when he looks at it, shall live. So Moses made a bronze serpent, and put it on a pole; and so it was, if a serpent had bitten anyone, when he looked at the bronze serpent, he lived*" (Num. 21:8-9). Brass or bronze speaks of judgment in Scripture. The altars of sacrifices and lavers (wash basins of water) of Moses' Tabernacle and Solomon's Temple were made of brass or bronze. They were placed in the outer courts where sin was dealt with before the priests entered the Holy Place where all the furniture was golden. Moses probably learned to forge metal from his brother-in-law, Hobab, or his father-in-law, Jethro (Num. 10:29, Jdg. 4:11). They were Kenites, a clan of metal smiths known for their craftsmanship.[91] Remember, Aaron fashioned the golden calf from smelted jewelry (Ex. 32:1-4). Both brothers were apparently skilled metal smiths. When the bitten Israelites looked at the brazen serpent, the venom lost its potency.

- **Christ's Comment:**

Jesus told Nicodemus about 1400 years later, "*As Moses lifted up the serpent in the wilderness, even so must the Son of Man be lifted up, that whoever believes in Him should not perish but have eternal life*" (Jn. 3:14-15). Why did Jesus compare Himself to a vile snake—chiefly an emblem of evil? Because He was going to become sin on the cross for us. "*For He made Him who knew no sin to be sin for us, that we might become the righteousness of God in Him*" (2 Cor. 5:21). Like a sponge, He absorbed our lust, pride, greed, hate, selfishness, jealousy, and bitterness. The poison of sin has infected us all, but Jesus provided the antidote. When we look with repentance and faith to the cross, the venom of sin loses its power.

Recently, a hiker was bitten by a rattlesnake. He was out in the middle of nowhere but, fortunately, he had an antivenom kit in his backpack. It saved his life. A doctor estimated by the fang marks that it was a mature snake and that he would have never survived without it. The blood of Jesus is our antivenom to sin. Keep your eyes on Jesus, keep your focus on the cross—that's your source of salvation and victory!

An interesting segue to this story involves Hezekiah, the thirteenth King of Judah, who led a spiritual revival and a crusade against idolatry about 680 years after Moses made the brazen serpent. People had started burning incense to and worshipping the old relic as an idol. Hezekiah, in righteous indignation, destroyed it—*"He ... **broke in pieces the bronze serpent that Moses had made**; for until those days the children of Israel burned incense to it, and called it Nehushtan"* (2 Kgs. 18:4). Nehushtan simply means "a piece of brass." Hezekiah was saying, "You're worshipping a piece of brass; it has no supernatural powers. It is merely an instrument God once used." Here we find a valuable spiritual lesson: Don't worship the instruments God uses; worship the God who uses the instruments. He has the real power! We often put people on an idolatrous pedestal by adoring celebrities, movie stars, singers, musicians, athletes, politicians, and even ministers. They are merely human vessels just like us. If you look to people, you will be disappointed. Keep your focus on Christ (Heb. 12:2).

A sculpture combining the brazen serpent and the cross by Italian artist Giovanni Fantoni stands on Mount Nebo, the site where Moses viewed Canaan Land before he died. Indeed, the cross is our passport to the Promised Land. There are also two icons used for medicine: the Caduceus symbol (two snakes intertwined on a winged pole, often used on pins for medical school graduations) and the Rod of Asclepius (one snake wrapped around a pole, used as logos on ambulances and hospitals).[92] While they originate from Greek mythology, they still point back to Moses' brazen serpent, which points us to the cross. Now, we don't look to a fake snake on a stake for help and healing; we look to the living Son of God. Look with faith and live!

PART 4

Inspired Insights on Various Biblical Themes

Chapter 27

Heaven—
Don't Miss It for the World!

What is heaven? Heaven is defined as "the dwelling place of God, the angels, and the spirits of the righteous after death."[93] Figuratively, heaven is a place or state of supreme happiness. When someone dies, we often use the cliché, "They're in a better place." However, heaven is not just a "better place"—it's the best possible place! Jesus promised, *"In My Father's house are many mansions* [dwelling places] ... ***I go to prepare a place for you****. And if I go and prepare a place for you, I will come again and receive you to Myself; that where I am, there you may be also"* (Jn. 14:2-3). Christ has been preparing that place for 2,000 years (what a place it must be). He is also preparing us for that place. So, heaven is a prepared place for a prepared people.

What are the three heavens? Paul spoke of being caught up into the "third heaven" (2 Cor. 12:2-4). The first heaven is the atmosphere around the earth (where birds fly, clouds form, and winds blow). The second heaven is outer space (the vast, galaxy-filled universe of planets and stars). The third heaven is God's dwelling place (paradise—where God, angels, and the spirits of redeemed saints live).

Where is heaven? God only knows. The Bible does not specify a place you can pinpoint on a map or with GPS. When Jesus ascended into heaven, He went UP (Ac. 1:9-11) and when He returns, He will come DOWN (1 Th. 4:16). Is heaven up geographically or dimensionally, or both? Heaven knows. Wherever it is, you can't reach it in a rocket (no astronaut has ever seen it from space). You can only reach it by faith in Christ via the rapture or resurrection.

Is heaven literal or spiritual? Yes, it is both! Heaven is a literal place we will enjoy in the future, but it is also a higher dimension we can experience to some degree now. Paul indicated that we are seated together "*in the heavenly places in Christ Jesus*" (Eph. 2:6). In a spiritual sense, the Kingdom of Heaven is wherever God's presence manifests and the King is in authority. So, spiritually speaking, when we are born again and submit to the King, we are translated into and can live in His heavenly kingdom/realm (Col. 1:13). Being a Christian means experiencing a foretaste of heaven here in this life. Of course, at the resurrection, we will experience and enjoy heaven literally in its totality.

What will heaven be like? The best description of heaven in the Bible is in Revelation chapters 21-22, but it isn't called "heaven." Instead, John the Revelator used four analogies comparing heaven to earthly things we can relate to and imagine:

1. **A City: New Jerusalem**—Rev. 21:2, 10-21.

When God moves to earth, He is bringing a whole new city with him. This massive city (1,500 miles long, 1,500 miles wide, and 1,500 miles high, bigger than half of the United States) will be a haven of rest eternally. Some say New Jerusalem is just the capitol city of a much larger heaven. Surely, it's the city that Abraham and the Patriarchs longed for—*"He looked for a city which hath foundations, whose builder and maker is God ... But now they desire a better, that is, a heavenly country. Therefore God is not ashamed to be called their God, for He has* ***prepared a city*** *for them"* (Heb. 11:10, 16). Old Jerusalem was David's capitol where he moved the Ark of the Covenant and where Solomon built the Temple (God's headquarters on earth). Ironically, Jerusalem means "possession of peace,"[94] although it's been a very war-torn city. Muslims, Jews, and Christians, all claim it as their spiritual capitol. New Jerusalem will dwell in permanent peace because the Prince of Peace will rule over it. John described it is a majestic city with walls of jasper, gates of pearl, and streets of pure gold like transparent glass (Rev. 20:14, 18-21).

2. A Bride: The Lamb's Wife—Rev. 21:2, 9-10.

John also compared New Jerusalem to the bride of Christ. But Christ's bride is not just a building; His bride is His church (Rev. 19:7-9). A city consists of its citizens, not just its structures. You've probably heard Squire Parson's famous song "Beulah Land." The name "Beulah" means "married" and is found in Isaiah 62:4-5, "*You shall no longer be termed Forsaken … but you shall be called Hephzibah, and your land* ***Beulah****; for the Lord delights in you, and* ***your land shall be married****. For … as the bridegroom rejoices over the bride, so shall your God rejoice over you.*" Heaven is not really about mansions and gold; heaven is about a passionate, love relationship with our heavenly groom. This is a love story, a divine romance—the Creator of the universe is head over heels in love with us (His eternal bride). God is meticulously preparing heaven for us the way a bride prepares for her wedding day. Think of all the preparation that goes into a wedding: clothes, hair, make up, flowers, jewelry, nails, music, food, place settings, cakes, beverages, decorations, and much more. Endless preparation goes into every detail so when the bride strolls down the aisle, she looks her absolute best and captures the eye and heart of her groom. Heaven is not just a physical place but also a spiritual state of matrimony to our Maker for whom we are preparing (Eph. 5:25-27, 31-32). God is searching for a bride who is as in love with him as He is with her. That will be heaven!

3. A Tabernacle/Temple:

John also compared heaven to a Tabernacle—a place of perfect fellowship. *"Behold,* ***the tabernacle of God*** *is with men, and He will dwell with them, and they shall be His people. God Himself will be with them and be their God"* (Rev. 21:3). The main reason God created mankind was for communion, which was broken by Adam's sin. Ever since, God has been restoring it. Notice His purpose for building Moses' Tabernacle, *"Let them make Me a sanctuary,* ***that I may dwell among them****"* (Ex. 25:8). That wasn't fully realized in the Old Testament. There was always a barrier between a holy God and fallen man. Jesus removed the barrier, the veil was torn in two, and the relationship has been repaired. Now, God is not interested in merely visitation; He desires habitation. God doesn't want just visitation rights on weekends (church on Sunday); He wants full custody (a daily walk). Strangely, there will be no churches in heaven. *"But I saw* ***no temple*** *in it, for the Lord God Almighty and the Lamb are its temple"* (Rev. 21:22). We won't go to church in heaven on the sabbath; we will live in God's presence 24/7 in an eternal sabbath.

4. **A Garden:** Rev. 22:1-3.

John also compared heaven to a garden of perfect provision, an Eden-like paradise. Remember, God planted the Garden of Eden perhaps as an earthly version of heaven (Gen. 2:8). The pure River of Life will flow from God's throne to quench our thirst. Plus, the Tree of Life, the same food source Adam and Eve enjoyed, will bear twelve kinds of fruit continually to satisfy our hunger. Furthermore, its leaves will release healing and health to the nations.

There will be at least ten "No Mores" in heaven:

1. No more sea—Rev. 21:1.
2. No more death—Rev. 21:4.
3. No more sorrow—Rev. 21:4.
4. No more crying—Rev. 21:4.
5. No more pain—Rev. 21:4.
6. No more curse—Rev. 22:3.
7. No more night—Rev. 21:23; 22:5.
8. No more devil—Rev. 20:10.
9. No more evil—Rev. 21:27.
10. No more sickness/disease—Rev. 22:2.

Doesn't that sound like the kind of place you want live eternally?

Universalism teaches that everyone eventually goes to heaven. Many think that no matter how they live, or what they believe, or what religion they follow, they will make it. That's not what the Bible teaches. Don't be deceived, friend, not all roads lead to heaven (Jn. 14:6, Ac. 4:12). The Bible is crystal clear on who will and who won't make heaven their home (Rev. 21:8, 24, 27; 22: 14-15). Certainly, God wants everyone to go to heaven (2 Pt. 3:9), but none of us deserve it. The good news is He extended an open invitation to all—"***Whosoever will****, let him take the water of life freely*" (Rev. 22:17). Your free ticket has been bought and paid for by the blood of Jesus if you confess, repent, and believe (Rom. 10: 9-10, Eph. 2:8-9).

John Newton, author of the classic hymn *Amazing Grace*, wrote, "If I ever reach heaven, I expect to find three wonders there: first, to meet some I would not have expected to be there; second, to miss some I would have expected to be there; third, the greatest wonder of all—to find myself there!"[95] There is nothing in this world worth missing heaven for. Don't sell your eternal, heavenly heritage for a cheap, carnal counterfeit. Heaven—don't miss it for the world!

CHAPTER 28

Parallels Between Noah's Day and Our Day

Some say Noah's Ark and the Genesis flood are just Old Testament legends. However, Noah is mentioned eight times in the New Testament. Even Jesus referred to the flood as a literal event. In fact, He prophesied, *"But as the days of Noah were, so also will the coming of the Son of Man be. For as in the days before the flood, they were eating and drinking, marrying and giving in marriage, until the day that Noah entered the ark. And did not know until the flood came and took them all away, so also will the coming of the Son of Man be"* (Mt. 24:37-39).

History often repeats itself. What we learn from history is that we don't learn much from history. Humanity has fallen into the same spiritual state which caused God to send the Genesis flood.

Observe seven parallels between Noah's day and our day:

1. Population Explosion:

"When men began to multiply on the face of the earth ..." (Gen. 6:1). There are an estimated 7.9 billion people alive on this planet now. Globally, about 385,000 babies are born daily or 140 million per year.[96]

2. Ungodly Marriages:

"The sons of God saw the daughters of men ... and they took wives for themselves of all whom they chose" (Gen. 6:2). Marriage is honorable since God instituted it (Heb. 13:4) but these were polygamous and/or ungodly unions which grieved God. Same sex marriages do the same today, and just because they are legal, doesn't make them right in God's sight. True marriage has always been traditionally, biblically, and historically a union between one man and one woman.

3. Reduced Lifespans:

"My Spirit shall not strive with man forever ... yet his days shall be one hundred and twenty years" (Gen. 6:3). In Genesis 5, people lived over 900 years. In part due to man's tendency for evil, God drastically shortened his lifespan. While life expectancy in America averages about 78 years, many lives are cut short due to sickness, accidents, violence, addictions, and other self-destructive behavior.

4. Widespread Wickedness:

"Then the Lord saw that the wickedness of man was great in the earth" (Gen. 6:5). No new sins are being committed today, there are just more sinners alive at one time. Plus, technology has made sin convenient. Sins that used to hide in the shadows on back streets now parade proudly down main street. Jesus predicted, *"Because lawlessness will abound, the love of many will grow cold"* (Mt. 24:12).

5. Rampant Violence:

The antediluvian world was *"filled with violence"* (Gen. 6.11-13). Today, a tsunami of violence floods the news, TV shows, movies, video games, and society. Murder and violent crime rates are escalating in our angry, cruel culture.

6. Mass Deception:

Noah's peers were spiritually blind to looming judgment even though they were warned repeatedly. They carried on business-as-usual right until the deluge drowned them all. Many today are oblivious to both natural and spiritual dangers looming over the world, consumed with the cares of life, and ignoring God's call to repent and be saved.

7. God had a righteous remnant:

"But Noah found grace in the eyes of the Lord" (Gen. 6:8). Where sin abounds, grace does much more abound. It was a small minority, but God found favor and started over with eight people.

God always has a faithful few—*"Even so then, at this present time there is a remnant according to the election of grace"* (Rom. 11:5).

The main takeaway from this true story is simply—don't miss the boat! The ark is a symbol of salvation. If you're not safely in the ark of salvation, you will drown in sin. Noah's generation was indifferent, indulgent, and ignorant. They ignored God's warnings and were suddenly swept away. Unrepentant sinners are like a man who jumps from a 50th floor window. Halfway down, someone asks, "How are you doing?" He answers, "I'm doing fine so faaarrrr!" You may be doing fine now, but it won't end well if you're not saved. It pays to serve God. It pays to serve the devil too, but you won't like the paycheck—*"For the wages of sin is death, but the gift of God is eternal life in Christ Jesus our Lord"* (Rom. 6:23).

Noah was 500 years old when God told him to build the ark; he was 600 when the flood came (Gen. 5:32; 7:6). As "a preacher of righteousness" (2 Pt. 2:5), he spent 100 years building the ark and warning the wicked. Some wonder, how could a loving God drown all those 'innocent' people? First of all, they weren't so innocent as noted above. Secondly, God warned them by Noah, giving them ample opportunity to repent and be saved. People still reject God's offer of salvation today and will pay a terrible price. Hell is not full of people who

God rejected; hell is full of people who rejected God (Jn. 1:10-12; 6:37). It's not His will that any should perish but that all should come to repentance (2 Pt. 3:9). There's a universal invitation to salvation—*"Whosoever will, let him take the water of life freely"* (Rev. 22:17).

Even in judgment, God showed mercy. How? Methuselah was Noah's grandfather. His name means "flood at my death" or "it shall be sent (a deluge)."[97] Some scholars believe he died the very year of the flood. God revealed to Enoch that judgment was coming and so he named his son "Methuselah." His lifespan was the longest of any person in recorded history (969 years—Gen. 5:27). Even in judgment, God was extending mercy by giving mankind the maximum amount of time to repent.

God was the ARKitect (pun intended) of this floating zoo. He gave Noah the blueprint and every detail is significant. Noah's ark was one big ship with three levels. This speaks of the divine Trinity—one God who expresses Himself in three persons (Father, Son, and Holy Spirit). The ark was pitched inside and outside for waterproofing. We also have a double seal—the blood of Jesus and the Holy Spirit. Amazingly, this huge ark only had one small window in the top. God didn't want Noah looking down at all the suffering, He wanted him to look up to his source. Jesus reminded us, *"Now when these things begin to happen,* ***look up*** *and lift up your heads, because your redemption draws near*" (Lk. 21:28).

The ark only had one door. God gave Noah specific measurements for the ark and the window, but not for the door. Why? Because the door represents JESUS and there is no limit to His power to save (Is. 59:1, Heb. 7:25). Jesus said, "***I am the door.*** *If anyone enters by Me, he will be saved*" (Jn. 10:9). Jesus is the one and only door to salvation (Jn. 14:6; Ac. 4:12, 1 Tim. 2:5). Then God shut the door (Gen. 7:16). The door of grace is still wide open now, but the time will soon come when God will close it suddenly.

Noah didn't have to hunt down and trap all the animals. God drew them sovereignly at the right time. Likewise, His Spirit is drawing people into the ark of salvation in these last days. Yes, we must witness and share the Gospel but, unless God draws people, they won't respond (Jn. 6:44). Remember, the ark started in the plain, but landed on Mount Ararat (modern Turkey—Gen. 8:4). All the storms in our lives will only take us higher if God is the captain of our ship. Also, the ark did not have a rudder or steering wheel because God guided it by His own hand. If God is our pilot, He will lead us safely to our destiny (Ps. 37:23). Notice only one family was saved from the flood (Noah's). One family was saved from Sodom (Lot's). One family was saved from Jericho (Rahab's). When judgment falls in these last days, only one family will be saved again—the blood-washed, born-again family of God (1 Th. 5:9).

Remarkably, baptizing the whole world in water didn't cure the sin problem. Later, Noah's descendants did the same sinful things. God painted a rainbow in the sky, a token of His promise to never again destroy the earth by water. Next time, it will be with fire (2 Pt. 3:10-13). Water cleanses; fire purifies! Water baptism is important, but it is not a cure all. John the Baptist said, *"I indeed baptize you with **water** unto repentance, but He ... will baptize you with the Holy Spirit and **fire**"* (Mt. 3:11). John provided the waterworks; Jesus produced the fireworks! All of us, as believers, need the fire baptism of the Holy Spirit to transform us from the inside out (Ac. 1:4-5, 8). Are you saved? Are you ready to meet God? If you miss God's provision of salvation, you'll miss everything. *"What will it profit a man if he gains the whole world, and loses his own soul?"* (Mk. 8:36) The door of grace is still wide open. Friend, whatever you do, don't miss the boat!

Chapter 29

Identifying the Spirit of Antichrist

Many believe the Antichrist will be a literal, global leader, but the spirit of Antichrist already permeates the world with its corrosive influence. We need keen spiritual discernment to recognize and resist it. Jesus warned that the number one sign indicating His soon return is mass deception (Mt. 24:4-5). He predicted deception will be so rampant in the last days that even the elect would be deceived "if possible" (Mt. 24:24). Thankfully, those who live by biblical truth and listen to the Holy Spirit will not be deceived. Discernment is "the ability to distinguish right from wrong, good from evil, truth from error, to perceive, detect, or to recognize."[98] The more familiar we are with a genuine item, the easier it is to spot a fake. The more we know and love the true

Christ, the less vulnerable we will be to the spell of the Antichrist.

The term "Antichrist" is found five times in Scripture, all in John's letters (1 Jn. 2:18, 22; 4:3, 2 Jn. 1:7). It means "an opponent of the Messiah, one who stands against or in opposition to all Christ represents."[99] This Satanic spirit is the driving force behind the evil in the world. While the Antichrist will be a literal person, the Antichrist spirit influences religions, governments, education, literature, music, movies, entertainment, and society. The spirit of Antichrist is anti-God, anti-Bible, anti-prayer, anti-morality, anti-biblical marriage, anti-authority. John explained, "*This is the* ***spirit of the Antichrist****, which you have heard was coming, and is now already in the world*" (1 Jn 4:3).

Here's the million-dollar question—who is the Antichrist? The Bible doesn't reveal his identity, but it does provide insight into his nature and agenda. The reason the Bible discusses him is not to foster speculation about his identity but to warn us of his deception. Whenever a villainous leader rises to power, people wonder if he is the Antichrist. Some thought it was Hitler, Mussolini, Lenin, Stalin, Fidel Castro, Saddam Hussein, Osama Bin Laden, and many other infamous villains. In the 1980s, some swore Mikhail Gorbachev was the Antichrist due to the strange birthmark on his forehead. Others insisted it was Ronald Wilson Reagan because there were six letters in each of his names equaling

666. This kind of crazy speculation is futile. While the Antichrist could be alive and in power, the Bible states, "*he will be revealed in his own time*" (2 Th. 2:6). Meanwhile, it's more important to recognize the characteristics of the spirit of Antichrist that is working in the world:

1. **A demonic hatred against God and His people:**

John wrote of the Antichrist, "*It was granted to him to make war with the saints and to overcome them*" (Rev. 13:7). Because Satan hates God and can't touch Him, he attacks His people instead. The spirit of Antichrist fuels anti-Semitism and persecution against the church. History is soaked with the blood of martyrs who were killed for their love for and loyalty to God. The Pharaohs enslaved and killed Hebrews in ancient Egypt. The Caesars of Rome executed Christians for sport. Hitler exterminated six million Jews in his hellish death camps. The same sinister spirit spurs the racial hatred of white supremacists, the KKK, Neo-Nazis, Antifa, ISIS, jihadists, and other radical groups.

2. **Efforts to remove and replace God:**

Paul described the Antichrist as "*The son of perdition, who opposes and exalts himself above all that is called God or that is worshiped*" (2 Th. 2:3-4). Again, this spirit is against God and everything good. It's the spirit behind the efforts to remove "In God We Trust" from our currency, "one nation under God" from our pledge of allegiance, the Ten Commandments from courtrooms and classrooms, prayer before high school football games and other public events, nativity scenes from public squares, and anything else that honors God in society. Any person, religion, or belief system that denies Jesus is the Christ and physically came in the flesh, or reduces His role in salvation, or exalts man above God is Antichrist (1 Jn. 2:22; 4:1-3, 2 Jn. 7).

3. Lawlessness and anarchy:

Paul called the Antichrist "the man of sin" and "the lawless one" (2 Th. 2: 3, 8, 9). This spirit drives the anarchy we see erupting worldwide in crime, rioting, looting, violence, and rebellion against authority. It consumes outlaws who thrive on creating chaos and anarchists who seek to destroy the systems of civilized society.

4. Mass deception:

Paul warned about the Antichrist's deceptive sway, *"The coming of the lawless one is according to the working of Satan, with all power, signs, and* ***lying wonders****, and with all unrighteous* ***deception*** *among those who perish, because they did not receive the love of the truth, that they might be saved. And for this reason God will send them strong delusion, that they should believe the lie, that they all may be condemned who did not believe the truth"* (2 Th. 2:9-12). The masses are swallowing Satan's lies hook, line, and sinker (Rev. 12:15-17). Millions believe the lies of evolution, that abortion is not murder, that salvation is optional, that it's ok to get drunk, use drugs, and have sex outside of marriage. Many will believe the damnable lie that the Antichrist is God, and/or that they are demigods, which will usher in divine judgment (Dan. 7:24-27; 8:23-25, Rev. 20:10-15). Daniel 8:25 warns, "*Through his cunning he shall cause deceit to prosper under his rule ... he shall destroy many in their prosperity.*"

5. **Blasphemy against God and sacred things:**

"*And he was given a mouth speaking great things and blasphemies ... Then he opened his mouth in blasphemy against God, to blaspheme His name, His tabernacle, and those who dwell in heaven*" (Rev. 13:5-6). Blasphemy is "the act of cursing or reviling God, assuming to oneself the rights or qualities of God, or irreverent behavior toward anything held sacred."[100] People who constantly use profanity have a blasphemous spirit. This often manifests in movies, music, and shows which feature constant cursing and taking God's name in vain. Blessing should flow from our lips not cursing (Eph. 4:29-31, Jam. 2:8-11).

6. Idolatry/false worship:

There is a global war over worship, a spiritual tug-of-war for the souls of men. God commands our worship and Satan covets our worship. Spurgeon said, "Consider how precious a soul must be when both God and the devil are after it."[101] If Satan can't keep people in bondage to sinful lifestyles, he'll get them mixed up in false religions. Satan tries to prevent our worship, pervert our worship, and/or pirate our worship for himself. The Antichrist *"opposes and exalts himself above all that is called God or that is worshiped, so that he sits as God in the temple of God, showing himself that he is God"* (2 Th. 2:4). Jesus called this blasphemous act the "Abomination of Desolation" (Mt. 24:15, Mk. 13:14). He will deceive and coerce the masses to worship him and take his mark or face execution (Dan. 11:36-37, Rev. 13:15-16).

7. An ugly, beastly nature:

In Revelation 13:1-8, the Antichrist is portrayed as a hideous seven-headed, ten-horned beast that rises out of the sea of humanity. Heads and horns speak of kings or kingdoms in Bible prophecy, indicating that he will control many nations. The scary imagery is of a ravenous beast which survives by devouring other things. Daniel 8:23 (KJV) calls him *"a king of fierce countenance"* referring to his ruthless rule. This shows the ugly nature of man's kingdoms—cruel, corrupt, bloodthirsty, power hungry, brutal, barbaric, and savage. Man's kingdoms are built by conquest, war, and bloodshed, and on the sweat, tears, and taxes of their subjects. Christ's kingdom is built on the lamb-like nature of love.

The good news is there is a restraining force preventing the Antichrist and evil from taking over. *"And now you know what is **restraining**, that he may be revealed in his own time ... only **He who now restrains** will do so until He is taken out of the way. And then the lawless one will be revealed"* (2 Th. 2:6-8). Notice the personal pronoun "HE." That restraining force is the Holy Spirit in and through the church. He is using a righteous remnant whose prayers are delaying judgment and restraining evil. Don't be too worried about the mark of the beast, because we've already been marked with the blood of Jesus. Plus, symbolically, the name of Jesus is already written in our foreheads (Rev. 22:4). This is God's way of branding his children with His mark of ownership so there is no doubt to whom we belong. As John wrote and warned us of the spirit of Antichrist, he also prophesied our victory, *"You are of God, little children, and have overcome them, because He who is in you is greater than he who is in the world"* (1 Jn. 4:4). The Spirit of Christ in us is greater than the spirit of the Antichrist in this fallen world!

Chapter 30

Seven Words That Changed the World

It might surprise you to know the word "faith" is only mentioned two times in the Old Testament. There were many true believers back then, but they were the exception rather than the rule. Synonyms like "believe" and "trust" are found numerous times. Heroes of faith like Abraham, Moses, David, Daniel, and many others overcame their doubts and displayed great faith in God. The first time the word "faith" appears is a divine indictment against Israel for their lack of it, *"I will hide my face from them, I will see what their end will be: for they are a perverse generation,* ***children in whom is no faith****"* (Dt. 32:20). The main reason the Israelites were not allowed to enter Canaan Land and wasted forty years wandering in the wilderness was due to their unbelief (Heb. 3:19).

The next time the word "faith" surfaced was centuries later in the Book of Habakkuk, a minor prophet with a major message that is still relevant today. Inspired by the Holy Spirit, he prophesied of a New Covenant Age, *"For the vision is yet* ***for an appointed time****, but at the end it will speak, and it will not lie: though it tarries, wait for it …* ***the just shall live by his faith****"* (Hab. 2:3-4).

Those seven simple, yet profound words—"the just shall live by his faith"—lay dormant for over 600 years until the Apostle Paul quoted them in his letters (Rom. 1:17, Gal. 3:11). The writer of Hebrews, perhaps Paul, also reprinted this statement (Heb. 10:38). Notice Habakkuk's original quote included the personal pronoun "his." That's important because no one will make it to heaven based on another person's faith. We all must have our own personal encounter with Jesus; our parent's or preacher's faith is not sufficient for us. We must have our own individual salvation experience through faith in Christ (Rom. 10:9-10, Eph. 2:8-9). The old saying is true, "God doesn't have any grandchildren, just children."

Let's break down this powerful phrase: "The just" (those who are justified or declared righteous in the sight of God) "shall live" (become and remain spiritually alive) "by his faith" (belief and trust in God). In other words, the way we get saved is the way we stay saved. We become spiritually alive at new birth by faith in the finished work of

Christ on the cross. We remain spiritually alive by continuing to believe in His atoning sacrifice. The classic hymn says it well, "My hope is built on nothing less than Jesus' blood and righteousness, I dare not trust the sweetest frame, but wholly lean on Jesus' name ... On Christ the solid rock I stand, all other ground is sinking sand, all other ground is sinking sand."

This simple truth doesn't seem like a big deal to us today, but over 500 years ago, these seven words literally shook the church order and changed the world. In 1505, a German university student was approaching a town when a violent storm erupted. Lightning struck so close that the young man fell to the ground. Scared, he made a rash vow and desperately prayed, "Saint Anne, help me and I will become a monk."[102] True to his word, Martin Luther became a devout monk. He lived a life of extreme self-discipline and isolation in a monastery. He was a tortured soul who deprived himself of most earthly pleasures. He fasted, prayed, studied Scripture, embraced poverty and celibacy, and fulfilled every ritual of the church to the max. He even refused blankets in the winter, slept on the cold, hard ground and nearly froze himself to death, all in an effort to gain God's favor. Still, he couldn't remove his sense of guilt and unworthiness.

"At times, he was proud of his sanctity and said, 'I have done nothing wrong today.' Then the misgivings would arise. 'Have you fasted enough? Are you poor enough?'" He believed later in life that his extreme fasting regimen permanently damaged his digestive system. He later said, "I was a good monk, and I kept the rule of my order so strictly that I may say that if ever a monk got to heaven by his monkery it was I … if I had kept on any longer, I would have killed myself with vigils, prayers, readings, and other work."[103]

In 1515, Martin Luther taught a class on the Book of Romans that turned his theology topsy-turvy. Studying Paul's writings, he rediscovered a simple truth that was forgotten during the Middle Ages. "Night and day I pondered until … I grasped the truth that … through grace and sheer mercy, God justified us by faith. I felt myself to be reborn and to have gone through open doors into paradise. The whole of Scripture took on a new meaning … this passage of Paul became to me a gateway to heaven."[104]

Luther finally realized that keeping religious rituals and shunning sin is NOT the primary thing that makes us right with God; rather, simple faith in Christ imparts to us His righteousness (all our righteousness is like filthy rags—Is. 64:6). Works do not replace faith in justification; they are merely the evidence of genuine faith (where there is fire, there is smoke) because "*faith without works is dead*" (Jam. 2:17-26). In other words, true faith produces action.

Luther's "new revelation" was not well received. In fact, after nailing his ninety-five theses to the Wittenberg Church door in 1517, he was condemned as a heretic and ordered to recant. When he refused, his writings were banned and burned. He too would have been burned at the stake, but he escaped and later translated the Bible into German. God used Martin Luther to spark the Great Protestant Reformation that swept the world. Protestants worldwide owe him a debt of gratitude all because he boldly believed a simple truth—*the just shall live by his faith*. Those same seven words can radically change your life too … if only you believe. Thanks Martin Luther, you literally and figuratively nailed it!

Chapter 31

When God Put Himself in a Box

We often say "don't put God in a box" but, ironically, He put Himself in one for over 800 years. What we mean by that phrase is to take the limits off God and give Him freedom to work as He sees fit. In other words, let go and let God have His way. God didn't confine Himself inside a box completely, but for centuries most of how God expressed Himself and manifested His presence, power, and glory revolved around a small, single box.

God gave Moses the blueprint for the Tabernacle and all its furnishings on Mount Sinai (Ex. 25-31). The Ark of the Covenant was built in Exodus 37 in around 1447 B.C. It was housed in the Tabernacle of Moses for centuries and moved around during Israel's trek through the wilderness and the conquest of Canaan. During the times of the Judges, it settled in Shiloh and in Gibeah, then it was relocated to the Tabernacle of David in Jerusalem. Finally, it was permanently set in Solomon's Temple where it remained during the reign of the kings of Israel. Solomon's Temple was destroyed in 586 B.C. So, for roughly 861 years, most of what God said and did in the earth was connected to this golden box (but it was no ordinary box).

The Ark of the Covenant was the most sacred piece of furniture on earth and Israel's most prized possession. It was a visible icon of the invisible God. There are nearly 200 references to the Ark in the Bible proving its prominent role in Israel's history. The Ark represented God's tangible presence among His people and was, in essence, God's representative throne on earth. It was housed in the Holy of Holies, an inner sanctuary of Moses' Tabernacle. It was the centerpiece of Jewish life and the epicenter of Israel's religion and worship. A pillar of cloud by day and fire by night hovered over it during their trek through the wilderness to signify God's Shekinah glory—a Hebrew term that means "the One who dwells."[105] In transport or battle, the Ark was carried on the priest's shoulders in either the front or center of the tribes (Num. 10:33-36, Josh. 3:13-17; 6:6-20). The whole nation of Israel revolved around the Ark and the twelve tribes camped around the Tabernacle (three tribes on each side). This is symbolic of how God desires and deserves to be the center of our lives, as our number one priority.

God gave Moses a blueprint to build the Ark on Mount Sinai (Ex. 25:10-22). Every detail has spiritual significance. The rectangular, wooden box was overlaid with gold. The dimensions are given in Exodus 25:10, NLT—*"Have the people make an Ark of acacia wood—a sacred chest 45 inches long, 27 inches wide, and 27 inches high."* The Ark was rather small, but it packed a big punch. It was a small box, but a big God was behind it (little is much if God is in it). Dynamite comes in small packages. The wood speaks of the human nature; the gold speaks of the divine nature (both in Christ and in us). It had a golden crown (border) around the top which speaks of the kingship of Christ and the royalty of believers. Four golden rings on the corners speak of taking the four Gospels to the four corners of the globe. Two staves (poles) were used for transport, a reminder that we are pilgrims on a journey heading home and this earth is not our final destination. Two golden cherubim (angels) were mounted on top facing each other with their wings touching. The cherubim, always connected with God's presence and holiness, remind us that *"The angel of the Lord encamps all around those who fear Him, and delivers them"* (Ps. 34:7).

The solid, gold lid of the Ark was called the Mercy Seat. Notice it was not a judgment seat. God told Moses, *"You shall put the mercy seat on top of the ark ... and there I will meet with you, and I will speak with you from above the mercy seat"* (Ex. 25:21-22). The High Priest sprinkled it with blood seven times on the Day of Atonement annually symbolizing the total removal of sin. The Ark contained the two Tablets of Stone inscribed with the Ten Commandments. Once the blood was applied, instead of seeing Israel through the broken Law, God saw them through the blood, the same way He sees us now. The term "propitiation," used three times to describe Christ, comes from the Greek word *hilasterion* which means "atoning sacrifice or mercy seat."[106] So, Jesus is our substitute and mercy seat granting us acceptance from and access to the Father (Rom. 2:25, 1 Jn. 2:1; 4:10).

Think of how God's glory manifested through this small box:

- As priests carried the Ark into the Jordan River, the waters rolled back, and the Israelites walked through on dry ground—Josh. 3:13-17.
- The Israelites marched around Jericho for seven days with the Ark in front and then shouted and God crushed the massive walls like matchsticks—Josh. 6:6-20.
- With the Ark leading the way, Israel conquered thirty-one kings and their armies during the conquest of Canaan—Josh. 12:1-24.

- When the Philistines stole the Ark, they put it in their temple with their pagan idol, Dagon, which fell prostrate before the Ark. They set it back up, but the next day it fell down again, and its hands and head were severed—1 Sam. 5:1-5.
- While the Ark was in Philistine custody for seven months, God smote them with severe plagues—1 Sam. 5:6-12.
- In Bethshemesh, 50,070 people were slain when they foolishly opened the lid of the Ark—1 Sam. 6:12-20.

Small box, big God! *"And it came to pass, when the ark set forward, that Moses said,* ***Rise up, Lord, and let thine enemies be scattered****; and let them that hate thee flee before thee"* (Num. 10:35). As long as Israel was true to God, they were invincible; when they strayed, they were vulnerable. The same is true for us today. The Ark is a fitting type of Christ since the fullness of God dwelled in Him (Col. 1:19; 2:9). However, it can also be a type of the Church. Just as that sacred chest held the Book of the Law, the Ten Commandments, a golden bowl of manna, and Aaron's rod that budded, so we contain God's Word and the life-giving power of the Holy Spirit. One major difference is the Ark was only God's temporarily dwelling place; we are God's eternal dwelling place via the Holy Spirit (Jn. 14:16, 1 Cor. 3:16).

It was a time of great spiritual decline and moral decay in ancient Israel. Eli, the obese High Priest, was ninety-eight years old and blind physically and spiritually. His corrupt sons, Hophni and Phinehas, were *"sons of Belial"* who *"knew not the Lord"* (1 Sam. 2:12, KJV). "Belial," a biblical term meaning "worthless or wicked fellows,"[107] is also a title of Satan (2 Cor. 6:15). Eli's sons disgraced the priesthood and provoked God's wrath by their greed and immorality.

After 4,000 men died in combat against the Philistines, Israel took the Ark of the Covenant with them in the next battle for good fortune. They suffered a devastating defeat—30,000 men died, including Hophni and Phinehas, plus *"the Ark of God was captured"* (1 Sam. 4:11). When Eli heard his sons were dead and the Ark was stolen, he fell off his seat, broke his neck, and died. Then his daughter-in-law went into premature labor and died birthing a son she fittingly named Ichabod, meaning "the glory is departed from Israel" (1 Sam. 4:21). What happened to Israel can happen to a country, a church, or even an individual. Losing the Ark meant losing God's presence and favor for which there is no substitute.

Upon capture, the Philistines placed the Ark in their Temple of Dagon, a god of grain and fertility (1 Sam. 5). Many today make this same mistake, presuming the God of the Bible is just one of many other equal gods. The next day, Dagon, a half-fish, half-man idol, was lying prostrate before the Ark. They set it back up, but the next day it fell down again, and its head and hands were completely severed. That was God's way of saying "I AM the one true God and will not dwell in the same temple with idols." The Ark moved around various Philistine cities for seven months, but it only produced trouble. The same Bible that brings blessings to obedient believers warns of curses to disobedient unbelievers. Eventually, Israel reclaimed the Ark which David later put in his tabernacle in Jerusalem. Then Solomon placed it in his magnificent Temple and God's glory returned to Israel.

The church, due to compromise, has lost some of God's glory, but we can reclaim it. The enemy has tried to steal our most prized possession, but it can be restored through repentance and prayer. What was true in ancient Israel is true for America, the church, and individuals. Let's reclaim the lost Ark in our own lives and ask God to restore the glory to His church once again!

So, whatever happened to the Ark? After the destruction of Solomon's Temple in 586 B.C., it vanished from biblical history. We do know neither Indiana Jones nor the Nazis found it as is depicted in the fictional movie *Raiders of the Lost Ark*. Jewish tradition says either Jeremiah or King Josiah hid it in a cave to prevent desecration. Others believe the Babylonians looted it. Some believe it is still hidden beneath the Temple mount in Jerusalem. The last time it is mentioned in Scripture is in heaven (Rev. 11:19), but is that the same Ark or a heavenly prototype of an earthly replica? Did God cherish the Ark so much He raptured it? Only heaven knows. For now, its fate remains a mystery.

Jeremiah prophesied of a time when the Ark would not matter anymore, *"Then it shall come to pass, when you are multiplied and increased in the land in those days," says the Lord, "that* ***they will say no more, 'The ark of the covenant*** *of the Lord.' It shall not come to mind, nor shall they remember it, nor shall they visit it"* (Jer. 3:16). In other words, the Ark is now obsolete. Why? Because under the New Covenant, God's people are His dwelling place, His temple, and the Ark of the Covenant, in a spiritual and symbolic sense, abides in us. God did miraculous things through a box in Old Testament times, and He can also do great things in and through us now. So, don't put God in a box. He doesn't live in a box anymore; He lives in YOU!

CHAPTER 32

David's Deep Affection for the Ark

A major difference between King Saul and King David can be seen in how they treated the Ark of the Covenant. Saul basically ignored it, and he ignored God. In his forty-year reign, Saul only mentioned the Ark once (1 Sam. 14:18) when he wanted God to help him defeat his nemesis, the Philistines. He met with Samuel a few times after being anointed king, but rebellion led to his demise. David, by contrast, made the Ark a central part of his life and reign. In fact, when he became king, he said, *"It is time to bring back the Ark of our God, for* ***we neglected it*** *during the reign of Saul"* (1 Chr. 13:3, NLT).

Some people treat God like the paramedics—they only call when they have an emergency. Many people want to keep God at a safe distance (close enough to be saved, but far enough away to run their own lives). They want a Savior to bail them out of trouble but not a Lord to whom they must surrender control. A clever church sign read, "Don't social distance from God!" In other words, don't be like King Saul who only sought God when he needed help. Someone said, "We often treat Jesus the same way Saul treated David—we want Him to slay giants and sing evil spirits away but we don't want Him to be King." One of the first things David did as king was to relocate the Ark to Jerusalem, so it was close to his palace. David dreamed of building a temple to permanently house it, *"I am living in a beautiful cedar palace, but the Ark of God is out there in a tent!"* (2 Sam. 7:2, NLT) While the Prophet Nathan agreed it was a good idea, God vetoed the plan due to David's history of warfare and bloodshed. His son, Solomon, whose name means "peace,"[108] would later build God's Temple.

David was a true worshipper who wanted to be close to the Ark and God's presence. By moving the Ark to Jerusalem, David was saying, "God is important to me. Spiritual things are my top priority. I want to be as close to God as possible; sacred things matter in my life." It was his way of honoring and putting God first. While David's motives were right, the method was wrong. The first attempt to move the Ark was a fiasco ending in a funeral. They made the mistake of putting that sacred box on an ox cart (2 Sam. 6:3). Obviously, they didn't learn from the Philistine's and the Bethshemite's blunders that provoked God's wrath and resulted in plagues and 50,070 deaths (1 Sam. 5-6). God let the ignorant heathen treat the Ark as common cargo, but not His people who knew better. The priests were supposed to carry it on their shoulders whenever it was transported. They used a man-made cart instead of handling the Ark the right way. God's glory doesn't come through man's methods. Sacred things should not be treated carelessly or casually. The Ark (an icon of God's presence) was to be honored and reverenced.

David led a festive parade with music, singing, shouting, and dancing, but the celebration ceased when the cart hit a pothole and the Ark shook. Uzzah tried to steady it, but when he touched it, he was stricken dead. So, they parked the Ark at Obed-Edom's house for three months while they mourned and studied how to move it properly. Meanwhile, "*The Lord blessed Obed-Edom and his entire household*" (2 Sam. 6:11, NLT). Later, he was among those appointed to minister before the Ark continually in the Tabernacle of David (1 Chr. 16:4-6). He wasn't satisfied with a short-term visitation; he desired long-term habitation.

Then David presided over a second procession to bring the Ark to Jerusalem (2 Sam. 6:12-23). This time the priests hoisted it high on their shoulders as God required. David could have sat in his palace and dictated and spectated. Instead, he participated. He didn't act stoic or dignified. He got so excited he couldn't contain his joy and broke out in extreme worship and *"Danced before the Lord with all his might; and David was wearing a linen ephod"* (2 Sam. 6:14). Notice David removed his fancy, kingly attire and put on an ephod (a priestly garment). He didn't sit on his throne and tell people how to worship, he shed his regal robes and showed people how to worship by example. David put his position and pride aside to exalt Yahweh—the true KING of Israel. His actions said, "I'm not the focal point here, it's not about me today. I will worship the great God of Israel without hesitation or reservation." David is a fitting type of Christ who laid aside His heavenly throne, and divested Himself of His heavenly garments, to become our heaven-sent High Priest.

Moving the Ark to Zion was a glorious event for Israel. Most people were thrilled, especially after receiving gifts from the king—bread, meat, and wine (their ancient stimulus checks—2 Sam. 6:19). But naysayers will always rain on your parade. Sourpuss Michal, King Saul's daughter and David's first wife, watched through her window with disgust and despised him in her heart (2 Sam. 6:16). She wanted her husband to act like a *king* not a *priest*! Kings rule, priests serve. She was ashamed of him because he didn't act very dignified. Our ego wants us to act like kings—show everyone who's boss, bark out orders, and make others serve us. God wants us to be priests—remove our phony facades and serve Him and others. Are we kings or priests? Do we demand that people serve us or do we serve them? Do we act like celebrities, thinking it's all about us? Or do we, like David, recognizing it's all about HIM?

Notice Michal's words dripping with sarcasm, *"How glorious was the king of Israel today, uncovering himself today in the eyes of the maids of his servants, as one of the base fellows shamelessly uncovers himself!"* (2 Sam. 6:20) She made it sound like he was prancing around naked, but he was clearly wearing "a robe of fine linen" (1 Chr. 15:27). She wanted him to act like a proud king, but David dressed and acted like a humble priest. If you get too extreme praying or praising God, people will criticize you. Remember, Mary poured her alabaster box of ointment on Jesus and the disciples threw a fit. David responded, *"I will be even more undignified than this, and will be humble in my own sight"* (2 Sam. 6:22). In modern slang, "Girl, you ain't seen nothing yet!"

The Ark arrived in Jerusalem—it's home for the next 456 years until Solomon's Temple was destroyed in 586 B.C. David made Zion his political capitol and the spiritual epicenter of Israel (God's headquarters on earth) by bringing the Ark and setting up a new Tabernacle. Unlike Moses' Tabernacle which revolved around sacrifices, rituals, and ceremonies, David's Tabernacle was based upon continuous worship. In fact, he appointed Levites to minster before the Ark around the clock (1 Chr. 16:1-6, 37). There apparently was no veil in David's Tabernacle, no barrier to hide the Ark. It speaks of New Testament worship which grants us unlimited access into God's presence by the blood of Christ. The modern worship music movement is a trend David pioneered 3,000 years ago.

So, what is our affection focused on? Spiritual, heavenly things or carnal, earthly things? Paul wrote, "*Set your affection on things above, not on things on the earth*" (Col. 3:2, KJV). David's affection was aimed at the Ark of God and the God of the Ark. If David held such deep affection for a golden box, shouldn't we fall in love with what that box represented—the presence and glory of our Lord and Savior, Jesus Christ?

Chapter 33

Was David Really a Man After God's Own Heart?

The Bible calls David "a man after God's own heart" twice. The first time was by Samuel who anointed him as backslidden King Saul's successor, *"But now your kingdom shall not continue. The Lord has sought for Himself a man after His own heart"* (1 Sam. 13:14). The second time was by the Apostle Paul who recounted Israel's history, *"I have found David the son of Jesse, a man after My own heart, who will do all My will"* (Ac. 13:22). What does it mean to be a person after God's own heart? Does it mean perfection? Certainly not! Nobody is perfect, except Jesus. Consider eight major mistakes on David's record:

1. **Fibbing to Ahimelech:**

David lied to the priest in Nob when he fled from Saul claiming he was on a secret mission for the king—1 Sam. 21:1-9.

2. Fleeing to Gath:

To escape Saul's wrath, David fled to Gath, the hometown of Goliath, (carrying the slain giant's sword was not a good idea). When he was recognized, he faked insanity to avoid capture, torture, and death—1 Sam. 21:10-15.

3. Fighting for the Philistines:

For sixteen months, David was a mercenary for Israel's enemy. Strangely, he wrote no Psalms during this period as the well of inspiration dried up.

4. Flubbing the transport of the Ark:

The Ark was handled carelessly and carried on a cart, instead of on the priest's shoulders, resulting in Uzzah's death—2 Sam. 6:1-10.

5. Falling into adultery:

His most famous failure was his scandalous affair with Bathsheba.

6. Finishing off Uriah:

Worse than his adulterous affair, was the subsequent cover up—the murder of Bathsheba's husband, Uriah the Hittite—2 Sam. 11:1-27.

7. Failing as a father:

David failed to discipline his son, Amnon, for raping Tamar, his half-sister. This led to Absalom's rebellion who murdered Amnon in revenge and then tried to steal David's throne.

8. Focusing on numbers instead of God:

Late in life, against Joab's advice, David insisted on counting his army (his 1.3 million troops were a source of pride and false security). This displeased God who sent a plague which killed 70,000 men—2 Sam. 24:1-25.

Obviously, being a person after God's own heart doesn't mean perfection or David would have been disqualified. In fact, with his rap sheet, he should have been dethroned, banished from Israel, executed for adultery and murder, separated from God, and damned eternally. That is what he deserved. Instead, he was forgiven, restored, allowed to stay in power, given an everlasting covenant, included in the lineage of Jesus, and was promised to reign again as a prince with Christ in the millennial kingdom (Ezk. 34:23-25). So, how do we explain all this? MERCY and GRACE! Mercy is when God does not give us what we deserve; grace is when God gives us what we do not deserve!

Why was God so merciful when David messed up so royally? First, because he genuinely repented (Ps. 51). Second, David was merciful to Saul when he could have killed him on several occasions. However, he refused to lift his hand against "God's anointed." Third, David was merciful to Absalom when he attempted a coup. Fourth, David showed kindness to a crippled man named Mephibosheth (Jonathan's son and Saul's grandson) and let him live in the castle and eat at his table as one of his own sons. David showed and sowed mercy, and when he needed it the most, it returned to him like a boomerang. *"Blessed are the merciful, for they shall obtain mercy"* (Mt. 5:7).

So, how can we honestly say David was a man after God's own heart? Because he was hungry for God, he sought after God, he had a passion for spiritual things, and he tried to please God despite his failures. His actions and words proved he was a God chaser:

- **He penned at least 73 psalms of worship.** He may have also written some of 49 anonymous Psalms; these lyrics express his deep desire for God and his heart-felt worship.
- **He positioned the Ark in Jerusalem.** By doing so, he made Jerusalem God's headquarters on earth. He loved God's presence so much he wanted to be as close to it as possible.
- **He provided a new tabernacle to house the Ark.** This replaced Moses' Tabernacle and revolved around true worship rather than sacrifices and rituals—2 Sam. 6:16-17.
- **He promoted musicians and singers to full-time worshippers.** Since he couldn't personally worship God 24/7, David delegated others to help him do it—1 Chr. 16:1-6, 37.

- **He proclaimed his desire to build God a permanent temple.** He felt guilty for living in a cedar palace while the Ark stayed in a tent and told Nathan his dream to build a temple—2 Sam. 7:1-14.
- **He planned and funded the Temple.** When God refused for David to build the Temple because he was a man of war and bloodshed, he stockpiled materials for Solomon (a man of peace) to build it.
- **His "perfect heart" (KJV) never turned to idolatry.** Most of the forty plus kings of Israel and Judah, including his own son, Solomon, fell into idolatry; David never did—1 Kgs. 11:4.
- **He was a pioneer in worship.** David was a man before his time (a New Testament man in an Old Testament era). He started worshipping Yahweh as a shepherd boy on his harp while tending sheep. God noticed and promoted him from the pasture to the palace where he revolutionized musical worship.

Truly, David was a man after God's own heart! Notice how God let him eat showbread (reserved only for priests) and wear an ephod (a vest-like priestly garment) when he danced before the Ark. Usually, God kept the kingship and priesthood strictly separated. In fact, King Saul was rebuked for offering sacrifices (1 Sam. 13:7-14) and Uzziah was stricken with leprosy for burning incense (2 Chr. 26:16-21). But David was a type of Christ who is both our King and High Priest, who has called us to reign with Him as kings and priests (Rev. 1:6; 5:10). David expressed his passion for God, *"My soul follows hard after You"* (Ps. 63:8). The Message reads, *"I hold on to You for dear life!"* David was truly a God chaser, *"As the deer pants for the water brooks, so pants my soul for You, O God. My soul thirsts … for the living God"* (Ps. 42:1-2). He knew the secret of running toward God instead of running from Him. David was far from perfect, but his heart kept pursuing the only One who is.

Chapter 34

The Curse That God Reversed

"*And God said to Balaam, you shall not go with them; you shall not curse the people, for they are blessed*" (Num. 22:12). Obviously, our enemy wants to curse us, but God intends to bless us. Balaam learned the hard way that you can't curse what God has blessed. It will roll off like water off a duck's back.

When Balak, the King of Moab, heard how the Israelites defeated the Amorites, he feared he was next on their hit list. So, he hired Balaam, a soothsayer from Pethor in Mesopotamia, to come and curse them. Pethor was a hub of oriental magic, a region famous for soothsayers. Balaam was later slain for his corruption and his ties to the Midianites, who were enemies of Israel (Num. 31:8, 16, Josh. 13:22).

Balaam was a curious mixture of good and evil, part sheep and part wolf. Herbert Lockyer wrote,

"Balaam had a head full of light but a heart that was dark, and great was the darkness."[109] Another commentator suggests, "As Judas was among the apostles, so Balaam was among the prophets, a true seer but a bad man."[110] In short, he was a false prophet whom God strangely used to prophesy some amazingly true things about Israel.

Three times Balak promised Balaam gold and glory in exchange for cursing Israel, but each time God gave him remarkable words of blessing over them instead. Initially, God told him not to go, but greedy Balaam stubbornly persisted. If you don't think there is comedy in the Bible, read the account of Balaam's talking donkey—or as I call it, the fool and his mule (Num. 22:21-34). When his donkey saw an angel with a drawn sword blocking the path, it went berserk and crushed Balaam's foot against a wall. Terror stricken, it eventually sat down and wouldn't budge. Balaam beat the donkey with his staff until he saw the angel too, then he fell on his face in repentance.

Incredibly, God used this crooked psychic to pronounce several lofty and true prophecies. For instance, he predicted Israel would rise up like an invincible, young lion (Num. 23:24). As long as Israel was true to their covenant with God, they were invincible. No enemy could stand against them and win. This prophecy, while spoken over Israel, can apply to us as well. As long as we remain faithful to God, *"No weapon formed against you shall prosper"*

(Is. 54:17). *"If God be for us, who can be against us?"* (Rom. 8:31) God has called the righteous to be as "bold as a lion" and to imitate the lion-like nature of Christ—the Lion of the Tribe of Judah (Pr. 28:1, Rev. 5:5).

Balaam further said of Israel, *"He bows down, he lies down as a lion; and as a lion, who shall rouse him? Blessed is he who blesses you, and cursed is he who curses you"* (Num. 24:9). You've heard the slogan, "Don't mess with Texas!" Balaam was warning the enemy, "Don't mess with Israel! If you pick a fight with God's people, you're picking a fight with God—a fight you will lose." Balaam even went on to predict the coming of the Messiah, *"A Star shall come out of Jacob; a Scepter shall rise out of Israel"* (Num. 24:17). Every time he opened his mouth to pronounce a curse, God reversed it, and it came out a blessing.

Unable to curse Israel, Balaam tried another strategy as his dark side reared its ugly head. The Moabites were known as "the people of Chemosh" (Num. 21:29), a pagan idol to which child sacrifices were offered, and they incorporated perverse sexual practices in their worship. So, Balaam counseled Balak to entice the Israelites into immorality and idolatry, knowing this behavior would grieve God and cause them to bring a curse on themselves (Num. 25:1-3; 31:16). Incidentally, Balaam's name means "devourer or destroyer of the people"—a fitting description of this devious man's diabolical deeds.

For those who might think Balaam and his animated donkey are just characters in an ancient fable, notice he is mentioned as a literal person three times in the New Testament by three different authors, all of whom condemned his actions:

1. **Peter called him a false teacher by saying,** *"They have forsaken the right way and gone astray, following the way of Balaam the son of Beor, who loved the wages of unrighteousness; but he was rebuked for his iniquity: a dumb donkey speaking with a man's voice restrained the madness of the prophet"* (2 Pt. 2:15-16).
2. **Jude compared him to backsliders who** *"Run greedily in the error of Balaam for profit"* (Ju. 11).
3. **John considered him a corrupter of Israel, similar to false leaders in the church at Pergamos,** *"Because you have there those who hold the* ***doctrine of Balaam****, who taught Balak to put a stumbling block before the children of Israel, to eat things sacrificed to idols, and to commit sexual immorality"* (Rev. 2:14).

If you re-read the timeworn tale of Balaam in Numbers 22-25, you'll learn several valuable lessons: First, while the enemy wants to curse you, God intends to bless you. Second, be careful about whom you allow to influence you. A soothsayer and immoral people lured Israel into sin. Third, don't be motivated by greed. The love of money led Balaam into all sorts of bad behavior. Fourth, even a donkey knows that you can't curse what God has blessed. What the enemy intends as a curse against you, God can and will reverse it and turn it into a blessing.

Chapter 35

Comparing Two Icons of Freedom

The Statue of Liberty is an icon of our political freedom.

The Cross is an icon of our spiritual freedom.

The Statue of Liberty was a gift from France to seal national friendship.

The Cross was a gift from God to seal divine sonship.

The Statue of Liberty features a female figure of the pagan goddess *Libertas* (the goddess of Liberty who was widely worshipped in ancient Rome, especially among freed slaves).[111]

The Cross featured a male figure of Jesus Christ—the visible form of the invisible God, the Author of Liberty, who is worshipped worldwide, especially among freed sinners.

Lady Liberty is clothed with a flowing gown (sculptures of Roman goddesses were often partly or totally naked).

Christ was stripped naked so we can be clothed with His royal robe of imparted righteousness.

A crown of seven spikes or sun rays form a halo on Lady Liberty's head representing the seven seas and/or the seven continents.

A crown of thorns formed a halo on Christ's head representing the curse of sin He bore for us.

A torch is in Lady Liberty's right hand representing the light of freedom and enlightenment.

Nails pierced Christ's hands—the true Light of the World.

A tablet in Lady Liberty's left hand is inscribed with the date July 4, 1776, to signify America's birthday.

Our name was inscribed in Christ's palms to indicate our spiritual rebirth day (*"See, I have inscribed you on the palms of My hands"*—Isaiah 49:16).

Under Lady Liberty's foot is a broken shackle and chain which represents the broken chains of tyranny and oppression and the abolition of slavery.

At the foot of the cross was a crushed serpent's head representing the deliverance from slavery to sin, self, and Satan (Gen. 3:15).

The pedestal on which the Statue of Liberty is mounted has a hallow rock containing a copy of the Declaration of Independence.

The Cross is spiritually anchored to the unshakeable rock of God's Word—the declaration of His truth and our dependence upon Him. "On Christ the solid rock I stand, all other ground is sinking sand!"

The Statue of Liberty is an icon of hope and freedom for millions of immigrants who pass through New York Harbor, the gateway to America, a passport to start a new and better life.

The Cross is an icon of hope and freedom for millions of sinners kneeling at Calvary, the gateway to heaven, the passport to start a new, abundant, and eternal life.

The song says it well, "As the statue liberates the citizen, so the cross liberates the soul. Oh, the cross is my Statue of Liberty, it was there that my soul was set free; unashamed I'll proclaim that a rugged cross is my Statue of Liberty!"

Consider this, if a false, pagan, Roman goddess can inspire hope and aspirations for political and social freedom to millions, how much more can the one, true, heavenly GOD (JESUS) bring hope and spiritual freedom to those who look to and kneel at the cross! We thank God for our political and national freedom but we thank Him even more for our spiritual freedom. As the Scripture inscribed on the Liberty Bell declares, *"Proclaim **liberty** throughout all the land unto all the inhabitants* *thereof*" (Lev. 25:10, KJV). The Cross is our true Statue of Liberty! "Though millions have come, there's still room for one. Yes, there's room at the cross for you." Let freedom ring!

Endnotes

1. Charles Spurgeon - All originality and no plagiarism makes for dull … (bibleportal.com), accessed 9/8/22.
2. George Sweeting, *Who Said That?* (Chicago: Moody Press, 1994), p. 61.
3. Ibid., p. 64.
4. Dictionary.com, accessed 10/13/22.
5. James Strong, *Strong's Concordance Hebrew and Greek Dictionary of the Bible*, on QuickVerse 10.
6. Ibid.
7. Ibid.
8. Dictionary.com, accessed 9/8/22.
9. Rich Strike wins 148th Kentucky Derby in stunning 80-1 upset (nypost.com), accessed 9/8/22.
10. Strong's, QuickVerse 10.
11. https://www.theverge.com/22250485/staples-easy-button-toy-commercial-design-user-interface-hack, accessed 9/8/22.
12. https://www.brainyquote.com/quotes/oprah_winfrey_133739, accessed 9/8/22.
13. Dictionary.com, accessed 9/8/22.
14. Strong's, QuickVerse 10.
15. Ronald F. Youngblood, *Nelson's Illustrated Bible Dictionary*, (Nashville: Thomas Nelson Publishers, 2014), p. 345.
16. Youngblood, *Nelson's Illustrated Bible Dictionary*, p. 509.
17. https://www.brainyquote.com/quotes/winston_churchill_103788, accessed 9/8/22.
18. Herbert Lockyer, *All the Men of the Bible* (Grand Rapids: Zondervan Books, 1958), p. 179.
19. Dictionary.com, accessed 9/8/22.
20. Strong's, QuickVerse 10.
21. *American Heritage Dictionary* (Boston: Houghton Mifflin Company, 1982), p. 306.
22. Youngblood, *Nelson's Illustrated Bible Dictionary*, p. 297.
23. Ibid., p. 629.
24. https://www.goodreads.com/quotes/654333-a-friend-in-need-is-a-friend-indeed, accessed 9/8/22.
25. Lockyer, *All the Men of the Bible*, p. 32.
26. Robert Young LLD., *Young's Analytical Concordance to the Bible* (Nashville: Tennessee Publishers, 1982), p. 14.
27. https://en.wikipedia.org/wiki/Whole_Lotta_Shakin%27_Goin%27_On, accessed 9/8/22.
28. https://www.newhealthadvisor.org/How-Many-Times-Does-Your-Heart-Beat-a-Day.html, accessed 9/8/22.
29. https://short-facts.com/how-many-miles-of-blood-veins-are-in-the-human-body/, accessed 9/8/22.
30. Albert M. Wells, Jr., *Inspirational Quotations* (Nashville: Thomas Nelson Publishers, 1988), p. 167.
31. Dictionary.com, accessed 9/8/22.
32. Strong's, QuickVerse 10.
33. Wells, *Inspirational Quotations*, p. 220.

34. Sweeting, *Who Said That?*, p. 458.
35. Dictionary.com, accessed 9/8/22.
36. *Reader's Digest Family Word Finder* (Pleasantville: The Reader's Digest Association, Inc., 1986), p. 888.
37. Charles R. Swindoll, *The Tale of the Tardy Oxcart*, (Nashville: Thomas Nelson Publishers, 1998), p. 625.
38. https://www.quotery.com/quotes/every-evening-turn-worries-god, accessed 9/8/22.
39. https://www.azquotes.com/quote/105858, accessed 9/8/22.
40. https://www.inspiringquotes.us/quotes/hm0k_TpfR5unh, accessed 9/8/22.
41. *Reader's Digest Family Word Finder*, p. 628.
42. Sweeting, *Who Said That?*, p. 206.
43. Ibid., p. 205.
44. https://www.goodreads.com/quotes/569716-blessed-is-the-person-who-is-too-busy-to-worry, accessed 9/8/22.
45. Youngblood, *Nelson's Illustrated Bible Dictionary*, pp. 458-459.
46. Dictionary.com, accessed 9/8/22.
47. Definition of Hebrew Names: Nimrod | AHRC (ancient-hebrew.org), accessed 9/8/22.
48. Youngblood, *Nelson's Illustrated Bible Dictionary*, pp. 131-132.
49. Wells, *Inspirational Quotations*, p. 62.
50. Lockyer, *All the Men of the Bible*, p. 87.
51. Ibid., p. 72.
52. Ibid., p. 136.
53. Paul D. Gardner, *Encyclopedia of Bible Characters* (Grand Rapids: Zondervan, 1995), p. 594.
54. Ibid., p. 472.
55. Ibid., p. 463.
56. Ibid., p. 66.
57. Ibid., p. 3.
58. Wells, *Inspirational Quotations*, p. 117.
59. https://www.brainyquote.com/quotes/john_c_maxwell_600892, accessed 9/8/22.
60. Dictionary.com, accessed 9/8/22.
61. Roberts Liardon, *God's Generals* (New Kensington: Whitaker House, 1996), pp. 182-183.
62. https://idioms.thefreedictionary.com/Bats+in+the+belfry, accessed 9/8/22.
63. Wells, *Inspirational Quotations*, p. 6.
64. https://www.brainyquote.com/quotes/martin_luther_king_jr_101472, accessed 9/8/22.
65. https://www.brainyquote.com/quotes/martin_luther_king_jr_297520, accessed 9/8/22.
66. Strong's, QuickVerse 10.
67. Dictionary.com, accessed 9/8/22.
68. Youngblood, *Nelson's Illustrated Bible Dictionary*, pp. 1203-1204.
69. Strong's, QuickVerse 10.
70. Youngblood, *Nelson's Illustrated Bible Dictionary*, p. 451.
71. Ibid., p. 66.

72. Strong's, QuickVerse 10.
73. Youngblood, *Nelson's Illustrated Bible Dictionary*, p. 517.
74. Ibid.
75. Bill O'Reilly, *Killing Jesus* (New York: Henry Holt and Company, 2013), p. 122.
76. Ibid.
77. Dictionary.com, accessed 9/9/22.
78. Youngblood, *Nelson's Illustrated Bible Dictionary*, p. 161.
79. Jamie Buckingham, *The Truth Will Set You Free But First It Will Make You Miserable* (Altamonte Springs: Creation House, 1988).
80. Herbert Lockyer, *All the Parables of the Bible* (Grand Rapids: Zondervan Publishing House, 1963), p. 9.
81. Strong's, QuickVerse 10.
82. Youngblood, *Nelson's Illustrated Bible Dictionary*, p. 851.
83. Ibid.
84. https://www.christianity.com/bible/dictionary/smiths-bible-dictionary/parable.html, accessed 9/9/22.
85. https://history.howstuffworks.com/historical-events/gettysburg-address1.htm, accessed 9/9/22.
86. Max Lucado, *No Wonder They Call Him Savior* (Multnomah Press, 1986), p. 31.
87. Strong's, QuickVerse 10.
88. https://bible.org/question/what-does-greek-word-tetelestai-mean, accessed 9/9/22.
89. Dictionary.com, accessed 9/9/22.
90. https://www.azquotes.com/quote/1170768, accessed 9/9/22.
91. Youngblood, *Nelson's Illustrated Bible Dictionary*, p. 652.
92. https://www.civilwarmed.org/caduceus-vs-asclepius/, accessed 9/9/22.
93. Dictionary.com, accessed 9/9/22.
94. Youngblood, *Nelson's Illustrated Bible Dictionary*, p. 583.
95. https://www.family-times.net/illustration/Gratitude/200005/, accessed 9/9/22.
96. https://en.wikipedia.org/wiki/World_population, accessed 9/9/22.
97. Lockyer, *All the Men of the Bible*, p. 329.
98. Dictionary.com, accessed 9/9/22.
99. Strong's, QuickVerse 10.
100. Dictionary.com, accessed 9/9/22.
101. https://tollelege.net/2021/07/03/what-must-it-be-to-lose-your-soul-by-charles-spurgeon/, accessed 9/9/22.
102. Roland Bainton, *Here I Stand* (Nashville: Abingdon Press, 1950), p. 21.
103. Ibid., p. 45.
104. Ibid., p. 65.
105. Youngblood, *Nelson's Illustrated Bible Dictionary*, p. 1051.
106. Strong's, QuickVerse 10.
107. Youngblood, *Nelson's Illustrated Bible Dictionary*, p. 152.
108. Lockyer, *All the Men of the Bible*, p. 319.
109. Ibid., p. 64.
110. https://bible-history.com/faussets/b/balaam/, accessed 9/10/22.
111. Information on the statue of Liberty was gleaned from https://en.wikipedia.org/wiki/Statue_of_Liberty, accessed 6/29/22.

Other books by Ben Godwin

www.ingramcontent.com/pod-product-compliance
Lightning Source LLC
LaVergne TN
LVHW010055110826
845155LV00028B/348

* 9 7 8 1 9 4 9 2 9 7 8 6 7 *